MACROECONOMIC ADJUSTMENTS

PRINCIPLES OF ECONOMICS SERIES

under the editorship of

EDWARD AMES

INTRODUCTION TO MACROECONOMIC THEORY

Edward Ames, State University of New York at Stony Brook

INTRODUCTION TO INPUT-OUTPUT ECONOMICS

Chiou-shuang Yan, Drexel Institute of Technology

MACROECONOMIC ADJUSTMENTS

John A. Carlson, Purdue University

MACROECONOMIC ADJUSTMENTS

JOHN A. CARLSON

PURDUE UNIVERSITY

Holt, Rinehart and Winston, Inc.

NEW YORK   CHICAGO   SAN FRANCISCO   ATLANTA
DALLAS   MONTREAL   TORONTO   LONDON   SYDNEY

EDITOR'S FOREWORD

This volume is one of a series of short introductions to important topics in modern economics. The publishers and the editor have been impressed by the development of economic research over the past twenty years, and by the slowness with which many exciting new problems have become accessible to undergraduates and their teachers. It is not yet clear which parts of this new research will become the backbone of teaching programs of the future, but it is clear that important changes will occur. The publication of a series of short, paperback volumes should permit instructors to experiment with new course material in areas where existing subject matter seems dated. Such a series also encourages the participation of young and active scholars in the development of new course material, without forcing them to write long textbook manuscripts. The series as a whole will offer a balanced presentation of new and traditional course material in such a way as to make it easier for instructors to introduce to their students the leading ideas and methods of modern economic thought.

Stony Brook, New York
October 1969

Edward Ames

PREFACE

College students are great skeptics. They want to know why they should learn what the teacher thinks they should learn. In a course on economic theory, this reaction can come not only from students who have difficulty grasping the material and need a rationale for their lack of understanding but also from students who find the theoretical arguments all very obvious. Granted the assumptions, the conclusions follow logically. So what else is new?

People, not mathematical functions or geometrical relationships, run an economy. We all know this. The economic theorist knows it too, and his theories are developed from assumptions about human behavior within the confines of environmental constraints. And yet there is a gulf between the abstract world of economic theory and the real world of our own experiences, a gulf that can puzzle and frustrate the beginning student.

This book is designed to help the student realize that the gulf is bridgeable. This is accomplished by means of a classroom economy in which the students themselves participate as decision-makers. The economy is constructed on the basis of a simple model from macroeconomic theory. While participating in a classroom economy, the students are able (1) to observe their own behavior and (2) to attempt an explanation for the behavior of the economy. In this simple setting the gulf between the individual decisions and a theoretical explanation for why changes are taking place in the economy is not overwhelming. Once the student grasps this link, he is better able to see the point of economic theory and to proceed to more complex formulations. This book is thus an introduction to macroeconomics and to economic theory in general. Since it uses a game device, it can also be approached with a spirit of friendly competition to see who can best manage a firm in the classroom economy.

I have tried to keep the entire game "on the level." The game itself is an outgrowth of experimental work by Vernon L. Smith and myself. In such experiments, the subjects are frequently in ignorance (or actually misled) as to the purpose of the experiment. In a classroom, however, it is important that students understand the structure of the process and become aware of what is going on. For this reason, there is no separate manual for instructors. All of the instructions concerning the game are contained in the text itself.

Despite the somewhat unconventional approach, the subject matter in this book is the standard fare found in most elementary treatments of macroeconomics. The concepts of net national product, the consumption function, the multiplier, and the theory of income determination are all carefully developed. There are discussions of how an economist might infer consumer behavior from available data, how investment plans can effect net national product and vice versa, and how fiscal policy may be used and has been used to influence the economy.

The plan of this book is indicated by the chapter titles. Chapter 1 presents a general introduction; Chapter 2 is devoted to a few preliminary concepts; Chapter 3 specifies the structure of the classroom economy; and Chapter 4 discusses national income accounting. Chapter 5 introduces the theory of income determination and describes how to get the classroom economy into operation.

The Appendix to Chapter 5 is primarily for the instructor who directs the classroom economy. This represents a partial substitute for an instructor's manual but it is a manual that the students are free to read. Although the appendix sets out procedural guidelines for the instructor, he may be as uncertain as the students about what is going to happen. He may find, as the author has, that the operation of a classroom economy can be a learning experience for the teacher as well as for the students.

The analysis, however, has not been left completely unstructured. Chapter 6 contains a discussion of how to infer consumer behavior from available data. Chapter 7 turns to investment decisions and begins to explore relationships in business cycles and growth, that is problems encountered in the analysis of economic activity as an ongoing process. Chapter 8 deals with how government fiscal policies can influence the level of economic activity. Finally, Chapter 9 puts the material covered in perspective and gives some indication of how complications within the basic framework can be investigated.

While this book is designed to be used independently (or in conjunction with any standard text) it is part of a series. In particular, it is a way of leading up to the more formal material in Edward Ames' *Introduction to Macroeconomic Theory*. He and I are agreed that most teachers would find it easier to use this book first and Ames' book later.

A number of classes have served as "guinea pigs" for the material in this book and their reactions have generally been favorable. I am grateful to Dennis Weidenaar, Gary Holman, Ronald Genda, and Anthony Herbst for trying earlier versions of this manuscript with their classes and to Emanuel Jones for his efforts between a class and a campus computer. The experience and comments of users have been of immense help in pointing up weaknesses in earlier drafts and have led to considerable improvement. I am also indebted to my father, Valdemar E. Carlson, for his useful and detailed criticisms based on many years as a professor of economics.

I would appreciate additional reactions from users of the present version. There is no one best way to utilize this classroom economy, but greater experience will undoubtedly suggest modifications that can be more effective for particular kinds of classes under varying circumstances. Hopefully these suggestions can be imparted to future users.

My greatest debt is to Edward Ames, who initially encouraged me to undertake the writing of this book and who has patiently read and criticized earlier drafts. His assistance has been invaluable.

John A. Carlson

Lafayette, Indiana
October 1969

CONTENTS

1

INTRODUCTION

We all develop habits and routines. Day after day or week after week we do the same sorts of things. Periodically, however, the routines are interrupted. A boy discovers girls; a man wins the Irish sweepstakes; a baby is born; a family moves to a new community; a young woman goes to college. Whether the changes are important or trivial, adjustments are necessary before the individual settles into newly established routines. In some cases changes may be so frequent that almost constant adjustment is required.

Individuals are most aware of the necessity for adjustment in their personal lives, but society, too, is constantly adjusting to changing conditions. Of interest to economists are changes in technology, products, prices, and standards of living, as well as a number of other related adjustments. With childlike curiosity we ask why. Why are these changes taking place? What is the process by which society adjusts to these changes?

Social scientists — sociologists, historians, psychologists, anthropologists, political scientists, economists — all attempt in their own ways to understand the nature of people's interactions. The motivation of the scholar may be the desire to satisfy his own curiosity, or it may depend on the hope that his studies can somehow contribute to a more effective control of the social process. For example, if the causes of poverty and the likely consequences of proposed remedies were adequately understood, legislators and administrators could design, enact, and carry out policies that would substantially eliminate poverty without creating other serious repercussions. Whatever his motivations, the scholar seeks to understand the workings of the world he observes.

Observation and description are prerequisites to understanding, but it is not enough to tell others what has been seen, experienced, tasted, or heard. It is also necessary to formulate explanatory theories. A *theory* consists of a set of assumed relationships. If people behave in a prescribed manner within a specified environmental setting, predictable results will occur. A theory explains some set of events. For example, imagine observing that the wages of steel workers go up most at times when the price of tin cans is rising, and that these wages go up least at times when the price of tin cans is steady or is falling slightly. A number of hypotheses about pricing policies of businesses and about what determines the wage rates for workers can be assembled to explain the observed relationship between steel workers' wages and the price of tin cans.

If several different theories explain the same set of observations, the scholar tries to determine which theory is most in accord with what he observes. He tentatively accepts those hypotheses which he believes best account for the facts of experience.

The most generally accepted hypotheses find their way into textbooks, and students are taught that this is the way things work. But textbooks change — an observation that should cause a note of skepticism. The social sciences, as well as the physical sciences, are very much in the process of developing. Scholars in every field are adding to knowledge and are occasionally discarding once-acceptable hypotheses. This book contains conventional doctrine, that is, some theories that are generally accepted as explanations of the way an economy functions. It is even more concerned, however, with showing how such theories can be developed and hence how transitory they may be. With such a perspective, the student will be better able to understand and adjust his thinking in later life, if scholars develop better explanations for economic phenomena, and he will understand why textbooks must be rewritten for the teaching of new generations of students.

1 MICROECONOMICS AND MACROECONOMICS

Economists study the utilization of resources for the satisfaction of people's desires and needs. The term *resources* refers to *physical* resources, such as land, minerals, and man-made equipment, and to *human* resources, that is, the physical and intellectual capabilities of people. Studies by economists cover a broad range of topics from "how an individual budgets his own spending" to "problems of international trade and international finance." Economics may be classified in a number of ways. The subject is sometimes divided into problem areas, such as labor economics, government regulation of business, public finance, economic development, business cycles, and other areas. Or the division may be methodological, such as historical and descriptive, statistical, or analytical and mathematical. These categories are useful in tying together related interests; but no matter how the subject is divided, very few economists will fall into any neat compartment. Their interests usually overlap any artificial boundaries.

Economic theory distinguishes between *microeconomics* (derived from the Greek word *mikros*, meaning small) and *macroeconomics* (from the Greek word *makros*, meaning large). *Microeconomics* is concerned with many small units (persons and businesses) within the economy and how they interact to determine the prices and quantities of individual products. *Macroeconomics* deals more with conglomerates and large aggregates, such as the price level, national income, and unemployment.

These distinctions are best understood by example. The introduction of jet aircraft in the United States both increased the speed and lowered the costs of transporting people over long distances. What further impact did jets have on the U.S. economy? In the area of microeconomics, a transportation economist might look at the impact on companies in both the airline and the railroad industry. He could use his theory to explain how jets influenced the relative prices charged to air and rail passengers, the relative shift in employment from the railroad to the airline industry, and changes in the profitability of companies in the two industries. Microeconomics is thus a study of relative prices and the composition of production in relatively small sections of the economy.

An economist with interests in macroeconomics could argue that the introduction of jets raised the income of the entire country by using labor more productively in the business of transporting people and things. His argument about this and other overall impacts of jet transportation would draw on macroeconomic theory. In focusing on totals, such as total income and total employment, an economist does not concern himself with the changing composition within these totals. Thus, in macroeconomics the emphasis is on the determination of aggregates rather than of specific prices and quantities.

Consider all the business organizations, small and large, throughout the country. Some are growing rapidly, some are doing the same amount of business that they have done for several years, and some are about to go bankrupt. To a large extent, which businesses succeed and which fail depends on the capabilities of the managers and the nature of the products they are endeavoring to sell. But surely it is not mere chance that in some years very high percentages of firms grow and relatively few decline while in other years few expand and most find business to be relatively poor. It is unlikely that the capabilities of many managers and the attractiveness of their products change so markedly from year to year. But then why does business as a whole intermittently experience good times and bad times? This book introduces a macroeconomic theory that provides an explanation for this sort of phenomenon.

2   ECONOMIC THEORY AND INDIVIDUAL BEHAVIOR

Macroeconomic theory is often presented as if "the economy" is some impersonal entity that automatically adjusts in accordance with the theory; yet individuals make the decisions that bring about the changes. The student should try to understand the links between individuals and the state of the economy as a whole. One way to become aware of this interdependence is to put the student in the role of an agent who must make decisions and be held responsible for the consequences of his own decisions. This suggests a game which simulates the behavior of an economy.

The appropriate structure of the game depends on the objectives of the learning experience. Games can be based on political processes, on international negotiations, on union-management bargaining, or on the determination of prices of products under various conditions. Since the subject matter of this book is macroeconomics, a simple form of a macroeconomic theory has been used to design the structure of a classroom economy.

Instead of being asked just to imagine how such an economy might function, the students will actively participate in making the decisions that determine events within their classroom economy. The participants must look at what is happening now, form their expectations about what is going to happen in the future, and make their own decisions of what to do in light of their individual objectives. This will illustrate to the involved student the interaction between individual decisions and macroeconomic adjustments. It also provides a complete example of how national income accounts can be derived from the records of individual businesses.

Experience in the classroom economy will be integrated with macroeconomic theory in two steps. The first step is to develop an explanation for events as they unfold in the classroom economy. In developing this explanation, the student learns the essential features of the theory that was used to design the economy in the first place.

The second step is to ascertain the relevance of this theory to an understanding of events that occur in a real economy, the U.S. economy. Here the process by which the theory was developed becomes important in explaining the classroom economy. The student should consider carefully how he came to understand what was happening in his own classroom economy. How was it possible to decide which hypotheses best explained behavior of the economic units? This spirit of inquiry can and should be carried over to an analysis of reported events in the U.S. economy.

Later chapters will show how the simple macroeconomic theory used in formulating the classroom economy helps the student understand discussions of government policies such as whether or not taxes should be raised or lowered. At the same time, some of the limitations of this theory will be indicated.

Developing a theory is like formulating a strategy in a game. An experienced chess player is always asking himself *what would happen if* he were to make a contemplated move. Among the alternatives he chooses what he believes to be the best move, given his objective of winning the game. Similarly, an economic theorist asks himself *what would happen if* people's decisions were related in specified ways to observable events. Out of such analysis may come plausible explanations for actual facts of experience or interesting suggestions about how economic activities ought to be organized.

A major objective, therefore, in establishing a classroom economy is to provide a setting in which explanatory hypotheses can be put forth and tested against some artificial (but largely unambiguous) facts of experience, namely, the data generated by the classroom economy. Whatever happens, each student should seek explanations for what he observes. Why are there ups or downs in business activity? How can he account for behavior within his own economy?

In a very simple economy, answers can often be found; but *what would happen if* things were not so simple? Bit by bit the inquisitive mind can complicate the set of assumptions and work out the consequences of these complications. In the process he learns economics. As he checks his theoretical conclusions against what he observes in the world in which he lives, he develops a better understanding of how an economy functions.

2

PRELIMINARY CONCEPTS

The great diversity of economic activity and the myriad of events that take place in any society make sense to the observer only if he can put them into understandable categories. Otherwise, everything seems chaotic and un-related. It is the purpose of this chapter to introduce a set of concepts that will provide some perspective and terminology for the material that follows. The first two sections discuss the fundamental notions of products and markets; the last three sections are devoted to concepts that facilitate analysis of economic activity as an ongoing process. The relevance of these preliminary concepts will become increasingly apparent as the subject matter is developed in subsequent chapters.

1 PRODUCTS AND SECTORS OF THE ECONOMY

Things are categorized by common characteristics — paintings by a particular style, religions by a denominational covenant. Economists are concerned with the goods and services that are produced and distributed to individuals. The way these diverse products are classified obviously depends on the interests of the classifier. Someone interested in natural resources may look at goods in terms of their primary physical sources, whether they are made from wood, iron, or petroleum, for example.

The theory of income determination, which is first explained in Chapter 5, is one of the fundamental elements of macroeconomics. The theory gives an answer to the following question: What quantity of goods and services will be produced and purchased during any period of time? Consequently, it is useful to lump together all of those products whose purchases are influenced by common factors. How finely the categories are drawn depends on the degree of complexity desired in answer to the question. Three broad categories — goods for use by people (*consumer* goods), goods for use by businesses (*investment* goods), and goods for use by governments — are sufficient for an introductory treatment of the theory. In fact, in order to make the initial theoretical argument as uncluttered as possible, consideration of demand by governments will be deferred and attention first focused on questions of what would happen in an economy with only a household sector and a business sector. An explanation of this terminology follows.

THE HOUSEHOLD SECTOR AND CONSUMER GOODS

When people can and do choose their jobs from among those available to them and select their own spending patterns, these decisions exert an independent force on the outcome of economic processes. People generally spend money for the purpose of maintaining and entertaining members of their own family or household, and so all spending decisions made for the satisfaction of individual or family desires are said to come from the *household sector* of the economy.

The goods and services that the household sector purchases are called *consumer goods*. Thus, everything from coffee cups and cherry cobblers to haircuts and canasta sets are lumped into the category of consumer goods if bought by *consumers* (another name for buyers of goods and services in the household sector). To round out the terminology applicable to the household sector, note that the total spending by consumers for consumer goods is called consumption expenditures, or, more briefly, *consumption*.

THE BUSINESS SECTOR AND INVESTMENT GOODS

Every economy has productive resources: labor skills, manufactured equipment, and an endowment of natural resources. To produce the goods and services that consumers want and are willing and able to pay for, these productive resources must be organized and directed. The decision-making unit that provides this organization and direction is called a business or a *firm*. The spending decisions of the firm are oriented toward the purchases of resources which can be used to make products to be sold as profitably as possible. The influences on a firm's spending decisions are likely to differ substantially from the influences on a household's spending decisions. Therefore, spending by firms is treated as a separate category.

While a firm may buy equipment and materials, hire labor, and produce goods, the actual decisions are made by people. Those people will be called *managers.* They must make such decisions as what kinds and how much of various products to produce, what prices to charge, what combination of inputs to use in production, and hence how much labor, equipment, and materials to acquire. The function of a firm and the criteria for making these decisions are developed in any price theory textbook. In this book on macroeconomics all firms are lumped together into a *business sector.*

All of the buildings (sometimes called the plant), equipment, and inventories owned by the business sector are called *investment goods.* The term *investment* denotes purchases by firms of new buildings, new equipment, and additional inventories. *Investment decisions* are decisions about how much to spend for new investment goods. These sketchy definitions will be supplemented in detail later since the concept of investment is critically important in all but the simplest form of the theory of income determination.

2 MARKETS

The concept of a market is fundamental to the theory of how a free-enterprise economy operates. Although it is an abstract concept, it is perhaps best understood by reference to a few specific instances. Imagine a small village on the seashore where many of the men in the village are fishermen. When the boats are in, the fishermen exchange their catch in the fish market for the local currency. In this instance the market is in one place with a well-defined product and with readily identifiable buyers and sellers. Another example is the New York Stock Exchange or stock market. There, members of the exchange execute orders from thousands of persons throughout the country. Trading takes place in a single location, but the stock certificates of many different corporations are being bought and sold, and the buyers and sellers are not easily identified.

A market may be local and specific, or it may cover a wide area and a variety of products. How the boundaries of a particular market are defined depends on the problem being considered. One man considering buying a filling station may be interested in the market for Brand X gasoline in Harmony, Indiana. An economist for a large integrated oil company will be more interested in the market for all petroleum products in the United States. In this latter case, the product, the buyers, and the sellers are much more diverse and harder to define than the market that interests the man in Harmony; yet each can legitimately be called a market.

In any case, *markets must have buyers and sellers.* The buyers constitute the demand side of the market and the sellers are the supply side. Real markets involve institutional arrangements by which buyers can obtain the product from the sellers and the sellers can be paid by the buyers. Economic analysis is concerned with the quantity of the product that will change hands and the terms (the prices) at which the exchanges take place. The larger the variety of the products within a market, the more macro-economic is the analysis.

Real buyers and sellers in a market may behave in complicated ways. Economists assume, however, that the behavior of buyers and sellers can be simply described. The behavior of buyers is defined by a rule called *demand*, which asserts that at any given price there is a quantity of the product that buyers will purchase. The behavior of suppliers is defined by a rule called *supply*. Associated with any price is a quantity that suppliers are willing to sell. If the market works efficiently, a price is established at which the quantity of goods that buyers wish to buy is equal to the quantity that sellers are willing to sell. Trading then takes place at that price. Markets must take into account how buyers and sellers behave. In this sense, we say that supply and demand determine the price and quantity of goods exchanged in a market.

Our concern here will be with the broadest categories of markets; with markets for consumer goods, for investment goods, for labor, and for finan-cial securities. Figure 2.1 has been prepared to help organize thinking in

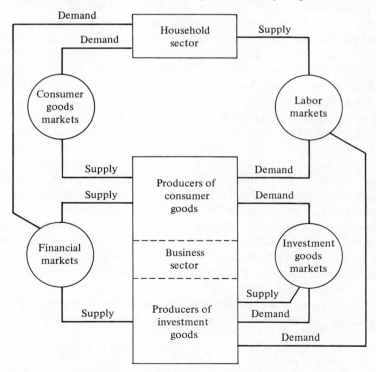

Figure 2.1   A Schematic Diagram of a Two-Sector Market Economy

these matters. The figure is a schematic diagram that provides an overview of the operations of a market economy in which there are only two sectors, a household sector and a business sector. In the diagram, a square box is a sector (a group of economic decision-makers), a circle is a market (in which goods and services exchange for money), and lines connecting sectors to markets are labeled either "supply" or "demand" in order to identify the sellers and the buyers in a market. The business sector has been divided into two parts: producers of consumer goods and producers of investment goods. Each of the four markets shown in the diagram will be discussed in turn.

Throughout most of this book, in fact until Chapter 9, possible influences that changes in the money supply can have on economic activity will be ignored. This does not constitute a denial of the importance of money. It simply allows emphasis on other aspects of macroeconomic theory. In the U.S. economy, *money* is usually defined as the sum of all demand deposits (checking accounts) in banks plus all paper money and coins outside of banks — in hands, pockets, purses, vaults, and so on. In general, money consists of anything widely accepted as a means of payment for other commodities. For example, a plumber is paid money for his services and then uses the money to buy such things as a new watch or a meal in a restaurant. Without this medium of exchange he might have to arrange to work for a jeweler, a restaurant owner, and other selected individuals in direct exchange for the things he wants. Details about how money comes into being are readily available in other sources.[1] Here the existence of money is taken for granted.

Consumer goods markets are depicted by the circle in the upper left-hand corner. The buyers of consumer goods are in the household sector. They come to the markets with a demand for, a willingness to buy, these goods. Hence, the line from the household sector to the consumer goods market is labeled "demand." The sellers of consumer goods are the firms in the business sector that are in the business of producing these goods. The line from the box representing producers of consumer goods to the circle for the consumer-goods markets is therefore labeled "supply." These markets may operate through many institutional arrangements, for example, department stores, neighborhood groceries, bars, mail order businesses, and automobile dealers. In the exposition of macroeconomics in this book all of these will be treated as parts of a single market for consumer goods.

Investment goods markets are shown in the lower right-hand corner of Figure 2.1. In order to produce goods that consumers wish to buy, firms

---

[1]A good source is "Modern Money Mechanics," a pamphlet from Research Department, Federal Reserve Bank of Chicago, P. O. Box 834, Chicago, Illinois 60690. *See also* Edward Ames, *Introduction to Macroeconomic Theory* (New York: Holt, Rinehart and Winston, 1968):pp. 72–76.

must assemble the necessary inputs. Various kinds of labor, materials, equipment, and buildings are needed; but materials, equipment and buildings themselves have to be produced. Thus, a firm that plans to manufacture and sell a plastic toy not only must hire labor but also must buy the plastic, or its ingredients, and the machines that form the toy. The willingness to buy these machines and materials is an example of the demand for investment goods. The firms which manufacture and sell such investment goods are designated in Figure 2.1 as producers of investment goods. They constitute the supply side of these markets. Producers of consumer goods are shown to be part of the demand for these goods. The rest of the demand comes from the producers of investment goods, since they, too, need to buy materials, equipment, and buildings in order to produce their output. These comments serve to indicate the interrelatedness of the business sector.[2]

Labor markets are in the upper right-hand corner of Figure 2.1. All producers need labor to create the products they hope to sell. They are willing to pay for these labor services and so come to the labor markets with a demand for labor. This is indicated in the figure by lines from both kinds of producers leading to the labor markets and labeled "demand." The household sector constitutes the supply side of these markets since individuals in the household sector sell the services of labor. Supply and demand determine the prices, in this case the wages and salaries, that are paid for various kinds of labor services. For the household sector, this is a major form of income that can then be used to buy consumer goods.

Financial markets, indicated by the circle in the lower left-hand side of the diagram, correspond to what are generally known as bond markets and stock markets. The role that financial markets play in the economy will be indicated only briefly here. Portions of Chapter 4 and Chapter 9 will go into somewhat greater detail.

When a business needs additional funds to buy investment goods, either it may borrow the money by issuing a bond or it may sell stock certificates.[3] A *bond* is a promise to pay a specified amount of money periodically and then to pay back the principal at some future date. For example, a bond might promise to pay $30 every six months and $1000 at the end of ten years. The payments of $30 are called *interest* payments. If the bond sells initially for $1000, then the buyer receives interest of three percent every six months, or approximately six percent per year. A *stock certificate* represents ownership in a business. If someone buys some stock in General Motors he becomes a stockholder, or part owner, of GM. In return for the

[2]Another volume in this series deals explicitly with such interrelatedness: Chiou-Shuang Yan, *Introduction to Input-Output Economics* (New York: Holt, Rinehart and Winston, 1969).
[3]It may also borrow from banks, but because money is not discussed in much detail in this book, this possibility is not considered here.

use of funds raised by issuing stock certificates, the business usually pays *dividends* to the holders of the certificates.

When a business obtains funds by selling bonds or stock certificates in order to buy additional investment goods, it does so in the expectation that the new investment goods will earn more for the business than they cost, so that the business can make the promised interest payments on its bonds and be able to pay dividends to the stockholders. In this sense, interest and dividends are payments to the household sector for the services of the investment goods that the business sector has acquired and uses.

To summarize:

> Households *buy* consumer goods
> securities (stocks and bonds)
> *sell* labor services
> Businesses *buy* labor services
> investment goods
> *sell* consumer goods
> investment goods
> securities.

Throughout the economy there is a flow of goods and services and a counter flow of money payments. The household sector receives income in the form of wage payments, interest, and dividends. People either spend this income on consumer goods or save it. The savings are then used by the household sector to buy stocks and bonds from the business sector.[4]

Economists are concerned with what influences the household sector's purchases of consumer goods and with what influences business decisions to purchase labor and investment goods, for these decisions determine people's incomes and the level of production of goods and services in the economy. Macroeconomic theory specifies how all of these decisions may be related.

3 FLOWS AND STOCKS

The treatment of time is an important matter in economic analysis. Since adjustments to changing conditions cannot be made instantaneously, some time must elapse before any adjustment can be completed. In fact, almost everything analyzed in this book will have some reference to time whether

---

[4]If the savings are used to increase the household sector's deposits in banks, it is convenient to think that the banks use these added funds to buy bonds or stocks from the business sector, so that the result is as if the household sector has indirectly acquired these securities.

or not the reference is made explicitly. Consider income. A man earns $100. Is this a large income or a small one? Obviously the question cannot be answered without additional information. Is the $100 the man's income for a year, for a week, for a day, or for an hour? In many countries of the world, the average income is equivalent to less than $100 a year. In the United States, an income of $100 a week is relatively modest. One hundred dollars a day is a very large income, and the man who continues to receive $100 an hour for his services can gross a million dollars in about five years (with a 40-hour week).

Technically, any magnitude that has a dimension per unit period of time is known as a *flow*. The term stems from the physical concept of a flow of liquid, which may be measured by the gallons of water *per hour* flowing into a reservoir or gallons of oil *per day* flowing through a pipe. As examples of economic flow variables, a man's labor services may be evaluated in terms of how many things he can make *per day* (piece rate) or how many hours he works *per week* (time rate). Just as income is defined in terms of time periods, so is a measure of people's purchases. The dollar volume of a family's expenditures for food, clothing, shelter, and other necessities, is meaningless unless related in some way to the period over which such spending takes place. All these examples are flows because they have a per-unit-of-time dimension.

A flow need not be continuous. The yearly flow of water into a reservoir may all come during a few months when the snow melts or heavy rains occur. An extreme example of a discontinuous flow is the interest payment on a bond. The bond may promise to pay the owner $25 every six months for ten years. The fact that payments come only at certain times should not disguise the fact that this is a flow, being a payment that occurs during an interval of time.

Another kind of magnitude is called a *stock*. It is a measure of something at a particular moment of time. The amount of water in a reservoir is a stock. A housewife keeps a number of cans of soup in her kitchen. The stock may vary from day to day or week to week, but *at any moment* she can count them and find that she has four, eight, eleven, or some other number of cans of soup on the shelf. In macroeconomic analysis one of the more important stocks is the stock of investment goods. The number and quality of the buildings, equipment, and unsold business inventories determine the productive potential of an economy. Examples are the number of lathes in a company's machine shop at *eight o'clock on a Monday morning* and the inventory of unsold Christmas-tree light bulbs in a department store at the *close of business on December 31, 1968*. Other examples of stocks, as well as flows, will appear as the subject of macroeconomics is developed.

In Chapter 3, two economic documents are discussed in detail. One is an income statement, the other a balance sheet. The income statement summarizes a firm's operations over a period of time, detailing its revenues, costs, and profits. All of these items are flows. Thus, income statements provide information about economic flows. The balance sheet records such things as the amount of cash a firm has, its holdings of investment goods, and its various debts at the moment of time the balance sheet is drawn up. This, then, is a document from which economists obtain information about the stocks within an economy.

4   PERIOD ANALYSIS

Clarity about dimensionality is important, but there is another compelling reason to stress time in a chapter on preliminary concepts. Economic activity is an ongoing process. Most people work because they know they will be paid for their services and can exchange their income for other things that give them satisfaction. The managers of a business enterprise hire workers to perform services that will create something of value to be sold profitably to prospective buyers. Whether the business builds bicycles, moves furniture, or turns out a newspaper, the managers expect that there will be buyers by the time the product or service is available. These decisions are made in the reasonably confident belief that the economy will continue to function in the near future in much the same way it has been functioning in the recent past.

Economic activity is a sequence of interrelated events. Decisions made at one time have their full impact only at a later time, and these effects in turn influence subsequent decisions. Thus, almost any event causes numerous ripples throughout the economy. An analytical device to organize thinking about time relationships is to divide time into a sequence of periods. At the beginning of a period decisions are made. During the period the consequences of the decisions are worked out. In light of these results, a new set of decisions must be formulated in the next period. And so on. While it may seem strange to assume that activity takes place in synchronized jumps from one period to the next, this may not be a serious distortion of what really goes on in an economy. It does allow for clear statements about antecedents and consequences in the process of economic evolution. This approach, known as *period analysis*, is used for the following reasons.

Production schedules are set and revised only periodically. For example, a meat-processing firm will usually guarantee its employees a number of hours of work for the coming week. This guarantee generally sets the amount of meat processing for the week since it would be uneconomical not to use the labor fully. During the week, as the managers become aware of any unanticipated changes in the demand for processed meat or in the supply of animals, they may plan accordingly to revise the guarantee of work either upward or downward for the following week. As another example, firms in the automobile industry set monthly production schedules that are met during the month (barring a major event, such as a strike). If sales are less than expected and inventories of unsold cars become excessive, production will be cut back in the following month, unless a very large pickup in demand is considered likely. Similarly, production will be increased in the following month whenever sales have been unexpectedly large and are expected to continue at this high level. In some instances, plan revisions may occur less frequently than every week or every month. Farmers, for example, plan most plantings on an annual basis. In any event, throughout the economy it is feasible to revise plans only on a periodic basis.

Data become available only periodically. There are weekly reports on the condition of banks' reserves. New-car sales are reported every ten days. Information about the cost of living, extent of unemployment, and industrial production is published on a monthly basis — often with a few weeks of delay after the end of the month. Preliminary estimates of the national income accounts are published quarterly, as are the reports of corporations' sales and profits. Economists seek to explain business activity and business decisions. But if decisions are made periodically and if information that helps businesses make decisions also appears periodically, then why should theories not also be cast in terms of events that take place in each of a sequence of periods? Ideally, of course, the data reported should correspond to the period over which decisions are not changed. The lag in information may even account for the fact that some decisions are changed only periodically, although this is not always true. In the case of the automobile industry, sales information is made available every ten days (about four days after the selling period has ended) while the production schedules are changed only monthly.

Finally, decisions take time to execute. When the managers of a company decide to order a new piece of equipment, the order can be placed immediately, but it may take several weeks or even months before the equipment is delivered. A professor may decide to adopt this book. Once notified of this decision, the bookstore orders an appropriate number of copies from the publisher. As soon as possible the publisher ships the books, but there will evidently be a delay between the decision to adopt and the immediate availability of the book to the students. There can also be secondary impacts. If this book is adopted in sufficient numbers, the publisher will schedule a new printing.

With the use of period analysis, economists may estimate how many periods it will take for the effects of certain types of decisions to be felt elsewhere in the economy and how soon there will be a reaction to these effects. The time dimension can thus be formally incorporated into economic theories.

5 EQUILIBRIUM AND STABILITY

The preceding sections have presented a few definitions and have discussed ways of cataloguing economic data and events. This section introduces a hypothetical state of affairs called a *stationary state*, which is a key concept in the theory of income determination, and one that proves to be useful as well in theories of macroeconomic adjustments. If taken literally the term stationary state can be deceiving. It does not mean that an economy has ground to a complete standstill, with all action suspended. It refers to a state of affairs in which no changes in actions are taking place from one period to another. Economic activity goes on in the stationary state, but it is completely repetitious. The income of the household sector, the consumer goods purchased, prices, techniques of production, and resources used are the same period after period. Furthermore, so long as nothing comes along to upset the balance, the economy stays in the stationary state. This has also been called the economy of the circular flow.

There is a similarity between this notion and the idea of physical equilibrium, in which a balance of forces holds an object immobile. The body of a helicopter hovering several feet above the ground is in equilibrium as the weight of gravity is exactly counterbalanced by the lift from the rotors. Unless there is a change in engine speed, or the wind, the helicopter will remain in the same position. An inflated ball floating in a small cove bounded by the sloping bank of a pond is held down by the force of gravity and suspended by the water. A trace of a breeze pushes against the ball and the bank resists the pressure. A balance of forces holds the ball in place until something in the environment changes.

In macroeconomics the stationary state is often called an *equilibrium* state of affairs. First the question is posed whether or not such a state of affairs can exist given the preferences of individuals and the motivations of business managers. If this question is answered affirmatively, the question of the stability of the equilibrium follows. Are there reasons to believe that economic forces will lead the economy to this state of affairs? Answers to questions of this sort depend on what influences the decisions of consumers, businesses, and governments, as well as the institutional and technological setting.

This ball analogy can usefully be pushed a step further. If lifted straight out of the water and released, the ball will return to its original position. The same is true if it were pushed under the water and released. With a small displacement out into the pond, the ball will be blown back to its cove by the breeze. If it is moved up the sloping bank it will roll back down. This property of returning to an equilibrium position when displaced is known as *stability*. Equilibrium is said to be stable whenever the object under consideration moves toward equilibrium from a position of disequilibrium, that is, when it is out of equilibrium.

The hypothesis, or often the belief, that economic agents force the economy toward a position of equilibrium, is at the heart of most treatments of macroeconomics. Of particular interest is the effect on the economy if conditions change slightly. In the physical analogy, if the pond recedes, the ball sinks. If the wind changes, the ball floats to another part of the pond. Economic analysis is often concerned with what will alter the conditions of the stationary state. How will a major invention or a shift in government policy change the equilibrium state of affairs? If equilibrium is always readily achieved, the process of moving from one equilibrium to another may be neglected; but if the process of moving generates pressures for further change, then the nature of the transition itself should be scrutinized. The title of this book, *Macroeconomic Adjustments*, has been chosen as a reminder of the importance of changes in any economy.

3

STRUCTURE OF THE CLASSROOM
ECONOMY

How does a group of individuals combine to form an economy? Are there predictable relationships among the parts of an economy? Consider an economy with (say) ten firms. This is small compared with a real economy. One is aware of all the firms in it. Will an economy with ten firms exhibit some of the characteristics of a real economy? We shall show that it can.

The class is to be broken into small groups with each group acting as a firm. That is, each is given a set of books similar to those of a business, only simplified. Each firm, acting independently, then makes a series of decisions. Consumers will behave in accordance with rules to be specified in Chapter 5. The teacher's function is to tabulate the firms' decisions and indicate the consequences of these decisions.

The rules governing decisions by both the business and household sectors will define the structure of a simple economy, called the classroom economy. This economy, patterned after the theory of income determination developed in this book, involves a number of simplifying assumptions about market behavior. The rationale for these assumptions will be presented subsequently when both the uses and limitations of the theory are discussed. The remainder of this chapter describes and explains key aspects of the classroom economy.

1   THE PRODUCTS

It is common practice in macroeconomic theory to put into one category all consumer purchases of goods and services. Consequently, the classroom economy is assumed to have a single, all-purpose consumer good that is capable of satisfying the needs and desires of the household sector. These goods will simply be called *consumer goods*, and the household sector will decide how many units of consumer goods they wish to purchase.

Students are going to manage firms that produce and sell consumer goods. As indicated in Chapter 2, firms generally need inputs besides labor services in the manufacture of their output. The producers of consumer goods in the classroom economy will need two investment-type goods, *materials* and *equipment*. The product called materials is used directly in the fabrication of consumer goods as is steel in automobiles or flour in bread. Equipment may be visualized as a long-lasting machine whose services are also used in the production of consumer goods.

There are thus three products in the classroom economy — consumer goods, materials, and equipment. The economy will be organized in such a way that all of the key decisions in the business sector are made by managers of the firms that produce consumer goods. They will order the necessary materials and equipment from other manufacturers and these other manufacturers will dutifully fill the orders. They must also try to anticipate consumer demand and make their production decisions accordingly. More will be said about this subsequently.

2   THE PERIOD

Period analysis, discussed in Chapter 2, assumes that decisions are made and revised only periodically. In an analysis of a real economy the period should be long enough for consumers to make and execute their spending decisions, for equipment and materials to be manufactured and delivered, and to justify making financial reports. At the same time, the period should not be so long that extensive revisions of plans can take place within the period.

For the classroom economy it is desirable not to proliferate the time dimensions of different activities, yet some link to calendar time provides a sense of concreteness. Therefore, a *month*, a well-defined unit of calendar time, has arbitrarily been chosen to be the length of the period. The production-decision period, the accounting period, and the length of delay between orders and delivery of materials will all coincide and be a month long. In discussions of the classroom economy, the terms period and month will be used interchangeably.

Just before a month begins, the managers of each firm producing consumer goods meet, review the current state of affairs, and make their decisions for the coming month. They place their orders for equipment and materials, set up the production schedules for the month, and hire the workers. Then production begins. Workers are paid, and people come in to buy available supplies of consumer goods.

At the end of the month, there are deliveries of the materials and equipment that were ordered earlier. Goods which cannot be sold are held as inventory until the next period. The managers figure the profitability of the month's operations and make their interest and dividend payments. They are then ready to place a new set of orders and make new production decisions. Thus the classroom economy moves forward through time from one month to the next.

3 PRICES, TECHNOLOGY, AND INITIAL CONDITIONS

The next few sections contain technical information about the classroom economy. For ease of reference a summary of the details can be found at the end of the chapter.

Prices

The following table gives the prices that will prevail:

Item	Price Per Unit in Dollars
Consumer goods	250
Labor services	100
Materials	100
Equipment	1200

Technology

Knowledge about possible techniques of production is known as the *state of technology*. Suppose the managers of a firm have decided how many units of consumer goods they are going to produce in the coming month. How much labor, materials, and equipment do they need or should they use in the production of this planned output? Quite often there is more than one way to produce a given output, with possibilities ranging from a great deal of labor and relatively little equipment to small amounts of labor and considerable equipment. The state of technology thus specifies all of the technical possibilities by which inputs can be transformed into outputs. The relationship that specifies how much output can be obtained from a given quantity of inputs is known as a *production function*. Of all the possibilities available to a firm, the managers select what they believe to be the economically most efficient one, that is the combination of inputs that can produce any desired level of output at the least possible cost.

In the classroom economy there will be only one known way to produce consumer goods, each unit can be produced with two units of equipment, one unit of labor services, and one unit of materials. For example, if the managers decide to produce 80 units of output, they will need 160 pieces of equipment, 80 units of labor, and 80 units of materials. This rigid relationship between inputs and output is known as a production function with *fixed proportions*.

Initial Conditions

In order to begin or continue operations and to plan intelligently for the future of the firm, the managers need to know where they stand whenever decisions are made. They should know the plant capacity (how much the firm can produce). They should know the costs and availability of other inputs, such as labor and materials. They should know the market prices of the items they sell and have some idea of the extent of the demand that can be expected in the future. They should know the stock of available inventories of materials, goods in process, and finished goods. Finally, they should know their financial position.

Some of these conditions have already been specified. The prices of consumer goods, labor, and materials are known and will remain constant. The extent of the demand for consumer goods is unknown at present, but managers will learn to gauge this fairly accurately when they have had some experience in running their firm. Some guidelines will be suggested in Chapter 5 before operations actually begin.

The stock of equipment is fixed at 200 units. Given the requirements of two units of equipment for each unit of output, the firm is unable to produce more than 100 units of consumer goods in any month. Its *capacity* is 100 units of output per month.

Every firm will begin the first month with the same stock of inventories: 100 units of materials and 25 units of consumer goods (unless the instructor chooses to specify a different initial holding of inventories). There are assumed to be no goods in process at the beginning of a month.

4 THE INCOME STATEMENT AND COSTS

The *income statement* provides a summary of the revenues, costs, and profitability of a firm's operations over a period of time. It is an economic document about flows. As such, its heading must indicate the period of time for which the report is made. This period is called the accounting period. The complexity of income statements varies from one company to another, but they all convey essentially the same sort of information. There is no need to go into great detail here, but an understanding of national income accounting, presented in Chapter 4, does require an understanding of the type of information contained in income statements. The following is always true by definition:

$$\text{Revenues from sales} - \text{Current costs} = \text{Net earnings}$$

Revenues from sales is self-explanatory. All of the income that the firm receives from the sale of its products goes into this category.

Current costs are all the costs incurred in making and marketing the products sold by the firm during the accounting period. They include costs of materials used in production, labor costs, costs of the services of plant and equipment, selling and administrative costs, and interest charges on the firm's debts.

The difference between revenue and costs is defined as *net earnings*. This is a measure of the firm's profitability for the accounting period. Out of net earnings, the managers decide how much to pay to the stockholders in dividends and how much to retain for reinvestment in the business.

The rest of this section discusses costs that firms in the classroom economy incur in addition to the costs of labor and materials. In Section 6 this information is put together to show how net earnings are computed for firms in the classroom economy, after Section 5 has introduced the concept of the balance sheet.

Depreciation Cost

In the classroom economy it takes two pieces of equipment to produce one unit of consumer goods. Each unit of equipment is worth $1200. Thus, $2400 worth of equipment is tied up for one month for each unit of consumer goods produced that month. At first glance it may seem strange that a firm can stay in business selling a unit of consumer goods for only $250 when it uses $2400 worth of equipment in producing the goods. The firm can stay in business because the equipment lasts for many months and can be used to turn out a large number of products before being scrapped. The $2400 can therefore be spread over many units of output.

The firm has 200 units of equipment worth $240,000. By the end of every month exactly $1200 worth of equipment is assumed to wear out and become useless. If this equipment were not replaced the firm would begin the next month with $238,800 worth of equipment ($240,000 less $1200). During the month the value of the equipment is said to *depreciate* by $1200. To the firm, *depreciation* is the value of equipment used up during the accounting period. The firm's financial records must allow for the cost of equipment used up. Thus, each firm producing consumer goods in the classroom economy will include $1200 per month for *depreciation charges* as one of its current costs.

Financial Cost

There is also a financial cost associated with owning equipment. When the firm acquires $1200 worth of equipment, it must pay the seller $1200, but where can the firm get the $1200 to pay for the equipment? Suppose the money is borrowed. When anyone borrows funds, he usually agrees to pay interest for the use of the funds. Let the going rate of interest be one percent per month. The borrower of $1200 for one month must then repay the lender the full loan of $1200 at the end of the month plus an interest charge of $12. It follows that an important cost of equipment can be the borrowing cost of the funds necessary to acquire the equipment in the first place.

This kind of cost, moreover, must be allowed for even if the firm does not have to borrow the money. Suppose a firm has $1200 in cash that is not needed for immediate expenses, such as meeting a payroll in a few days. Suppose that the cash can be used in one of two ways. It can be used either to buy a piece of equipment or to lend to some borrower at the going interest rate of one percent per month. If the firm lends the money, it earns $12 per month. If the equipment is purchased, the firm foregoes the opportunity to earn $12 per month. In buying the equipment the firm, in effect, has incurred a cost by choosing not to lend the money at the going rate of interest.[1] Such a cost must be weighed in any evaluation of how profitable it would be for a firm to acquire or continue to operate a piece of equipment.

The going interest rate will be one percent per month. The financial cost of owning $240,000 worth of equipment is, therefore, $2400 per month.

Inventory Holding Costs

There is one more cost to consider, the cost of holding inventories. The materials that a firm has available at the beginning of a month for use in production during the month were delivered and paid for at the end of the preceding month. The firm has paid for these inventories of materials and will not be reimbursed until the goods embodying the materials are sold. To simplify the record keeping, assume that the firm borrows the money it needs to pay for these materials at the end of one month and repays the loan, with

---

[1]This is an example of an *opportunity cost*, an important concept usually developed in price theory textbooks.

interest, at the end of the next month. The interest charges on the loan are the costs of holding materials in inventory.

There is a cost of holding inventories of finished goods as well as of materials. For each unit of consumer goods that has been produced and not sold, the firm has paid in direct costs $100 for the materials plus $100 for labor. Therefore for each unit of unsold consumer goods the firm must borrow $200. At an interest rate of one percent per month, each unit of consumer goods in inventory costs the firm $2. Each unit of materials in inventory costs $1 per month.

In ordering a supply of materials for next month's production and in scheduling production of consumer goods for the current month, the managers should take into account the fact that it does cost the firm something to hold inventories. There should be sufficient inventories to be able to meet demand, but beyond a certain point it is an unnecessary expense to carry extra units in inventory. The managers must decide where that point is and plan accordingly.

5 THE BALANCE SHEET

In Chapter 2, a distinction was drawn between flows and stocks. In this chapter the income statement has been described as an economic record of a firm's flows of revenues, costs, and earnings. The firm's stocks are described in a *balance sheet*.[2] It shows the stocks of things owned, the stocks of debts of the firm, and the stock of claims of the owners of the business. The balance sheet consists of two lists, which are referred to as sides, an *asset side* and a *liabilities-plus-net-worth side*.

All assets of a firm are stocks (that is, they are evaluated at a moment of time, have value, and are owned by the firm). Thus, in the classroom economy, the asset side of the balance sheet lists cash, inventories of materials, inventories of finished goods, and equipment. If buyers were allowed to charge their purchases, and some of the accounts had not been paid by the beginning of the month, there would be an asset called *accounts receivable*. Accounts receivable are claims to payment and they are of value to the firm (if payments are received eventually). Accounts receivable are only one example of many items that do not appear in the balance sheets of firms in the classroom economy but can be found in the balance sheets of actual businesses.

The liabilities-plus-net-worth side of the balance sheet lists the short-term debt, the long-term debt, and the net worth of the firm. All of these terms will be explained in conjunction with an illustrative balance sheet shown in Table 3.1.

[2]Do not confuse the technical term *stocks* with securities sold on stock exchanges.

Table 3.1   A Producer of Consumer Goods Balance Sheet, Beginning of Month 1

Assets		Liabilities and Net Worth	
Cash	$ 10,000	Short-term debt	$ 15,000
Inventories		Long-term debt	150,000
Materials	10,000		
Finished goods	5,000	Total liabilities	165,000
Equipment	240,000	Net worth	100,000
Total	$265,000		$265,000

Table 3.1 presents the initial balance sheet for every firm that produces consumer goods in the classroom economy. The first thing to note about this balance sheet is that it is dated, as all records of stocks must be dated. It is drawn up as of the beginning of month 1. If a new balance sheet were to be drawn up at some later month, it is very likely that each firm will have different numbers in its balance sheet.

The first item on the asset side shows a cash balance of $10,000. Additional cash will be received from the sale of consumer goods during the month, but money is needed to meet expenses, such as wages and salaries before the receipts come in. If the managers could estimate all the expenses that the firm will incur before income is received and hold only that amount of cash, any money in excess of those needs could then be used to reduce the firm's debt. Since we are trying to keep the managers' decisions as uncomplicated as possible, this possibility will not be introduced. Ten thousand dollars is assumed to be enough to bridge the gap between payments by the firm and the income from sales of consumer goods. Procedures will be set up so that the firm begins every month with precisely $10,000 in cash.

Inventories of materials are valued at their cost of $100 per unit. The firm begins month 1 with 100 units of materials, which have a total value of $10,000, as shown in Table 3.1. Unsold units of consumer goods are to be valued on the basis of variable production costs per unit. These costs, $100 for materials plus $100 for labor, total $200. Therefore, the 25 units of consumer goods in inventory at the beginning of month 1 are valued at $5000.

The last asset shown on the balance sheet is equipment, worth $240,000. Normally fixed assets such as buildings and equipment, are recorded on the balance sheet first in terms of their original cost and then the cumulative amount of depreciation is subtracted. The original cost and the amount of depreciation are generally both shown. In the classroom economy, however, any equipment that depreciates will be automatically replaced so that the value is always equivalent to the current purchase price of equipment.

Summing the value of the cash, inventories, and equipment gives a figure for total assets of $265,000.

Liabilities are items owed by the firm, that is obligations to make payments at some time in the future. The usual distinction between short-term liabilities and long-term liabilities is whether or not the obligation must be paid within a year. If it must be paid within a year, it is a short-term liability. Otherwise, it is a long-term liability.

In Table 3.1 short-term debt refers to the debts the firm incurs when borrowing to finance its inventory holdings. This debt must be paid back at the end of the month. As a general rule, it is not possible to look at a company's balance sheet and identify a liability item that matches an asset item. An exception to this rule occurs in the classroom economy since the short-term debt will always equal the value of the firm's inventory holdings. At the beginning of month 1, the firm's short-term debt is shown as a debt of $15,000.

The firm also has a long-term debt of $150,000 at the beginning of month 1. This represents money that was borrowed because the owners did not have enough money of their own or did not believe it expedient to deplete their own cash to pay the full cost of acquiring the firm's assets. The owners have agreed to pay the going rate of interest of one percent per month on this debt. The debt itself is due at some date well in the future and so is called a long-term debt. There is no need to be concerned with it here except to note that the firm is obligated to pay the interest cost of $1500 per month (1 percent of $150,000).

Total liabilities at the beginning of month 1 come to $165,000.

A firm's net worth is the value of the ownership of the firm. For example, suppose a young man's only asset consists of a $3000 automobile and his only liability is an unpaid balance of $2000 on a loan from a finance company. By subtracting his $2000 liability, the unpaid balance on the loan, from his $3000 asset, the young man's net worth can be seen to be $1000. If he could sell the car for $3000, he could pay off his loan and still be worth $1000. It is not usually true that a person or firm can liquidate or sell all assets, pay off all liabilities, and end up with the exact amount of net worth shown on the balance sheet. In principle, however, that is the idea of net worth. If the net worth of any firm in the classroom economy (or in real life) drops to zero, that firm is *bankrupt*.

Table 3.1 shows the firm with total assets of $265,000 and total liabilities of $165,000, leaving a net worth of $100,000. Thus, at the beginning of month 1, the ownership of the firm is valued at $100,000.

6   FINANCIAL RECORDS AND INVENTORY INVESTMENT

In the classroom economy, the accounting period, as well as the decision period, covers one month. At the end of each month managers are to compute the profitability of the firm's operations during the month. The structure of the economy allows for a very simple set of books. Costs conveniently fall into three categories: variable costs of goods sold, inventory holding costs, and fixed costs. The magnitudes of each of these costs can be explained with reference to the information presented above.

The only costs that vary directly with the production of consumer goods are the costs of labor and materials used in production. Each unit of consumer goods produced requires one unit of materials at $100 per unit and one unit of labor at $100 per unit. Thus, the *variable costs of production* come to $200 per unit of consumer goods produced.

Inventory holding costs take the form of interest charges that work out to $2 per unit of finished consumer goods and $1 per unit of materials. A firm that begins month 1 with 100 units of materials and 25 units of finished goods will pay $150 as interest on short-term debt.

Fixed costs are costs that the firm incurs no matter what its level of operation is. In the classroom economy these costs are interest charges on the long-term debt ($1500) and depreciation charges ($1200). These total $2700.

Now, for illustrative purposes, suppose that in month 1 a firm (1) orders 85 units of materials, (2) produces 85 units of consumer goods, and (3) sells 76 units of consumer goods. The firm is assumed to have the initial balance sheet shown in Table 3.1. Net earnings, shown in Table 3.2, will be discussed after an explanation of how to deal with changes in inventory.

Consider the example. There is no change in the inventories of materials. The firm uses and orders 85 units. There is, however, an increase of 9 units of finished goods in inventory since the firm produces 85 and sells only 76 units. Recall from Chapter 2 that investment goods include inventories held by the business sector. The value of the change in inventories is called *inventory investment*.

At $200 per unit, the costs of the 9 units added to inventory are $1800. Thus the firm *invests* (adds to its stock of investment goods) $1800 in inventories. By subtracting the $1800 spent for inventory investment from the $17,000 in expenditures for labor and materials, the accountant arrives at a figure of $15,200 for the variable costs of goods sold.

The same procedure works for changes in inventories of materials. Suppose, in the example, that the firm ordered 86 instead of 85 units of materials. It would therefore spend another $100 for materials but it would also add another $100 to its inventories. When the figure for change in inventories is subtracted from the costs of labor and materials, the two $100 entries cancel each other. The costs of goods sold is still $15,200 as it should be if the firm sells 76 units.

Inventory investment can be negative as well as positive. If more materials are used than are ordered there will be a decrease in the inventory of materials. Similarly, when the firm sells more units of consumer goods than it produces, the stock of finished goods in inventory goes down. In such cases the accounting procedure amounts to adding the value of these goods taken from inventory to other outlays in arriving at a figure for costs of goods sold.

If these adjustments for inventory changes were not made in the income statement a firm could show unusually large profits when it depletes its inventories and appear to be taking losses when it adds to its inventories even if it makes a good profit on each unit sold. In Table 3.2, for example, revenue from sales is $19,000 from selling 76 units at $250 per unit. Outlays for materials and labor come to $17,000. With no adjustment for inventory changes, and with the other costs, this firm would appear to have lost money in month 1 when, as we shall see, it is operating profitably.

Table 3.2   A Producer of Consumer Goods; Illustrative Income Statement, Month 1

Revenue from Sales			$19,000
Less:	Variable Costs of Goods Sold:		
	Materials	8,500	
	Labor Cost	8,500	
		17,000	
	Deduct: Change in Inventory	1,800	15,200
Gross Profit			3,800
Less:	Other Costs		
	Interest on short-term debt	150	
	Interest on long-term debt	1,500	
	Depreciation Charges	1,200	2,850
Net Earnings			950
Less:	Dividends		760
	Retained Earnings		190

Gross profit is defined here as the difference between revenue from sales and variable costs of goods sold. In the case illustrated in Table 3.2, the figure is $3,800. For actual record keeping in the classroom economy it is possible to obtain this figure more directly. Each unit of consumer goods sells for $250 and has a variable cost of production of $200. There is a gross profit of $50 per unit sold. When 76 units are sold, total gross profit is seen to be $3800 by multiplying $50 times 76.

The other costs, totaling $2850, are the costs of interest payments and depreciation charges. When $2850 is subtracted from $3800, the firm shows net earnings of $950.

The magnitude of the dividends to be paid to stockholders will be determined by a rule to be specified below. In the example for illustrative month 1, dividends are $760. With $760 paid out in dividends and with net earnings of $950, the firm has retained earnings of $190 as shown in Table 3.2. Retained earnings represent a change in the net worth of the firm.

In summary, the performance of each firm will be measured by a figure called *retained earnings*, which is computed by multiplying the number of units sold by $50 and then subtracting inventory holding costs ($1 per unit of materials and $2 per unit of finished goods), fixed costs of $2700, and dividends.

7 THE DECISION PROBLEM

The cost structure described above lends itself to the use of a chart, called a *breakeven chart*, that shows the relationship between volume of sales and the resulting profitability of the firm's operations. Refer to Figure 3.1. The number of units sold by one firm is plotted along the horizontal axis. Dollar values are plotted along the vertical axis. The line labeled Gross Profit represents the gross profit that would be realized at the corresponding volume of sales. Gross profit is $1000 at 20 units, $2000 at 40 units, and so on. Fixed costs in this figure are $2700 plus an allowance of $150 for inventory holding costs. Fixed costs are therefore drawn as a horizontal line at a height of $2850. Where the gross-profit line crosses the fixed-costs line is called the *breakeven* point. At this level of sales, net earnings are zero. With sales below this level net earnings are negative; with sales above this level net earnings are positive. The line labeled Net Earnings is obtained by taking the difference between the gross-profit line and the fixed-costs line. In this particular figure the breakeven point is shown to be 57 units. If inventory holdings were lower, the breakeven point would also be lower. For example, if inventory holding costs were only $100 instead of $150, it can readily be shown that the breakeven point would be at 56 units.

The firm is required to purchase $1200 worth of equipment every month so that it will always begin a month with precisely $240,000 worth of equipment and a capacity to produce of 100 units of output. This rule removes one complication from the managers' decision problem. They are not free to increase or decrease the firm's stock of equipment. What might happen if they were given this discretion is considered in Chapter 7.

The problem the managers face each period is to decide how many units of materials to order and how many units of consumer goods to produce. The objective of the managers will be to make the sum of their firm's re-

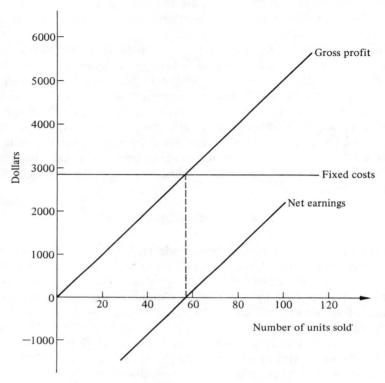

Figure 3.1   The Relationship between Sales and Earnings for a Firm in the Classroom Economy

tained earnings as large as possible while the classroom economy is in operation. This objective will be restated at the end of Chapter 5, after the forms have been discussed.

From what has been said about the profitability of the firm, the volume of sales is evidently of crucial importance. But what determines sales? This the managers must find out for themselves. Details on how to approach the problem will be given in Chapters 5 and 6. In each period managers have to form expectations or anticipations about how many units will be sold. These expectations can then be used to plan the levels of output and new orders in as profitable a manner as possible.

8   REVIEW AND SUMMARY

There are three kinds of commodities: consumer goods, materials, and equipment. Production decisions are made at the beginning of a month and are not revised until the beginning of the following month. Workers are paid wages, lenders receive interest payments, and owners of firms receive net earnings (whether paid out as dividends or retained and added to net worth). This income received by the household sector is assumed to influence the household sector's decisions to purchase consumer goods. In the course of a month, firms sell goods to consumers from the available supply. At the end of the month the profitability of each firm's operations is figured and a new set of decisions made for the following month.

All prices and costs will remain at the following levels:

Consumer goods	$250 per unit
Materials	100 per unit
Labor costs	100 per unit
Equipment	1200 per unit
Interest charges	1 percent per month
Depreciation rate on equipment	0.5 percent per month

Each unit of consumer goods produced by a firm during a month requires 2 units of equipment, 1 unit of labor, and 1 unit of materials. Since the firm has a stock of only 200 units of equipment, no more than 100 units of consumer goods can be produced in any one month (unless the teacher chooses to relax this rule).

Each firm borrows an amount equal to the value of its inventory holdings each month and has a long-term debt of $150,000. On both of these debts it pays an interest charge of one percent per month.

The information presented in this chapter will next be used to illustrate the construction of national income accounts (in Chapter 4) and then to introduce the theory of income determination (in Chapter 5).

4

NATIONAL INCOME ACCOUNTING

In Chapter 3 the accounting system of individual firms was described and in particular the simplified firms of the classroom economy were set up. In this chapter, we shall discuss how the data on individual firms are put together so as to provide information about the entire economy. This discussion will pertain both to the national income accounts of the U.S. economy and to what will be called the classroom income accounts of the classroom economy. Data contained in both kinds of accounts will be studied in more detail in later chapters.

Businesses in the United States employ economists to analyze past and impending changes in the national income accounts as an aid to the executives who make important managerial decisions. Managers in the classroom economy may similarly find clues in their official accounts about what to expect in the way of future changes in the fortunes of their own firms, and may thus be able to plan accordingly.

1 NNP AND GNP

The appropriate measure of how much has been produced over a period of time depends on the attitudes and values held by those who control the means of production within an economy. If a Pharaoh thinks that the building of a huge pyramid is the only important activity and effectively controls all labor within his jurisdiction, then total production will likely be measured by dimensions added to the pyramid during a period of time. The production of food would not be counted since the food is used solely to maintain workers' ability to work. The food is used up in the production of the "final" product, the pyramid.

Our concern in this section will be with developing a figure that reflects total production within a society in which the aim of all economic activity is to satisfy the needs and desires of its individual members. Whatever the length of the accounting period — be it a month, a quarter, or a year — we seek a figure for how much was produced during the period. This figure will be called *net national product*, frequently abbreviated to *NNP*.

Two questions immediately arise. Which products should be included and how should they be valued? Neither question is easily answered, but since a major purpose of this chapter is to convey the concept of net national product, many of the complicating details will be omitted and the answers given in relatively simple terms.[1]

Consider the valuation question first. Any first grader who has had the "new math" (and presumably any college student) knows that a set of apples cannot be added to a set of rides on a merry-go-round. A common yardstick, however, is provided by the market value of goods and services. If each apple is purchased for ten cents and each ride is purchased for fifteen cents, total expenditures for these items can be measured in terms of dollars. Therefore, dollar values will be used to add up the products included in the final total.

Two criteria will be used to determine whether or not a product is to be included in NNP: (1) It must be considered to be of value to members of the household sector and (2) It must not have existed (at least not in the same form) before the accounting period began. These criteria will be considered in greater detail as the major categories of NNP are discussed. Both must be satisfied.

All goods and services sold to the household sector are called *consumption expenditures* and are included in NNP. Consumer purchases of radios, clothes, meals in a restaurant, and taxi cab rides are all examples of consumption expenditures. They meet the first criterion, for if people buy these products willingly, they are presumably of value to the household sector.

The second criterion poses something of problem. Note the last word in the term *net national product*. The purchase of an item during an accounting period does not necessarily mean that it was produced during the period. A radio, for example, could have been sitting in a warehouse for a year before it was sold. The purchase of such a radio should not be, and in fact is not, included in net national product. It is not subtracted directly from con-

---

[1]More detailed analysis of U.S. national income accounts is given in Sam Rosen, *National Income:* Its Measurement, Determination, and Relation to Public Policy. (New York: Holt, Rinehart and Winston, Inc., 1963).

sumption, however, because the figure for consumption in itself is of interest to economists. The reasons for this interest will be developed in Chapters 5 and 6.

The adjustments are made in terms of changes of inventories in the business sector. Suppose a radio manufacturer begins a period with a stock of completed radios. Any radio sold from the stock to a consumer should not be in NNP. It fails to satisfy criterion (2), but any radio produced during the period should be added to NNP since, as we shall argue below, it can be said to be of value to the household sector. If there is no change in inventories of radios (that is, the flows of production and purchases are equal) then for every radio purchased another one has been produced. No further adjustment in NNP is necessary, since the production of radios is already in the consumption figure; but if the manufacturer ends the period with more radios than he began with, then consumer purchases of his product understate the actual production that has taken place. Similarly, if he ends the period with fewer radios than he began with, consumer purchases of his product overstate actual production.

Before saying that changes in business inventories should be added to NNP, we must decide whether or not these changes are of value to consumers. If our only interest in economic activity were in how many goods and services consumers acquire each period, then we could concentrate only on purchases of consumer goods. Our interest, however, is the amount of *production* for consumers. When production exceeds the consumption of some commodity, there is recorded an increase in unsold business inventories, yet the items are available for eventual sale. In a sense, people in an economy are better off, given their level of consumption, if the stock of business inventories has gone up than if inventories have not increased or have gone down. More can be made available for future consumption since resources can be devoted to producing other things in addition to the inventories already available. Thus, any change in business inventories is included in NNP.

This inclusion of changes in business inventories applies not only to finished goods but also to goods anywhere in the process of being manufactured. In order to explain why, it is useful to introduce the term *intermediate product*. An intermediate product is anything used up in the production of other products. As an example consider a magazine publisher. When a man buys a copy of the magazine, the cost of the paper is incorporated in the selling price of the magazine. The paper used in the magazine is an intermediate product. As with final products sold to consumers, there is no need to make any adjustment in NNP if the production of paper just equals the use of paper in the production of the magazine. If, however, the publisher has added to his stock of paper during the period, this increase in inventory is of value to the consumer in the same sense as the change in inventories of finished goods were said to be of value.

Intermediate products should not be added into NNP since they are already counted in the value of other products. To count both the purchases of the household sector from the publisher and the purchases of the publisher from the paper manufacturer would be to count the value of the paper twice, once when sold to the publisher and again as part of the sales of the magazine. Such *double counting*, as it is called, would clearly overstate the value of production.

Any increases in business inventories, however, are to be counted in NNP in that more has been produced than is recorded by the purchases of the household sector. In the sense that the business sector is the final purchaser of additions to inventories during the accounting period, they may be called final products. Note that if inventories should happen to go down this part of "final product" is negative, since in that case consumer purchases have overstated the production of goods during the period. Business inventories are one form of investment goods, that is, goods acquired by the business sector for the purpose of producing goods for the ultimate user, which in the U.S. economy is the household sector. Additions to the stock of investment goods are treated as final products.

The distinction between consumer goods and investment goods is often arbitrary. The purchase of a car for personal use is presently counted in the U.S. as a consumption expenditure, but it could be counted as the purchase of an investment good that provides services to the household sector. The services of the car then become the final product, which may be valued in terms of the portion of the value of the car used up during an accounting period. In the pyramid example, food was treated as an intermediate, not a final, product.

In any event, once the decisions have been made about what to count as investment goods and what to count as consumer goods, *all investment goods are eventually intermediate products*. Buildings and long-lasting pieces of equipment may not be readily perceived as being used up in production. Machines are used, for example, in the process of making shoes; and the cost of the machine's services is passed on to the buyers of the shoes as surely as the cost of the leather is in the final selling price of the shoes.

The difficulty is in valuing in any one period the services of a machine which has a useful life of a great many periods. The usual convention is to allocate a specified portion of the total cost of the machine to each period as the cost of having or using the machine during that period. This cost, as in the classroom economy, is called *depreciation* and represents a measure of the value of the services of the machine during the period. The treatment of durable equipment and buildings in the measure of total product is, in principle, the same as the treatment of business inventories. If the value of new buildings and equipment exceed the value of buildings and equipment used up, the economy's potential output in the future has been increased. This increase in the economy's stock of investment goods is thus of value to consumers.

To see this last point, imagine an economy that is capable every year of producing $200 billion worth of goods and services for consumers. Suppose with a slightly different organization of productive resources, the same economy in one year can produce $170 billion worth of consumer goods and add $30 billion worth of equipment to the present stock. In the following year the economy will then be capable of producing perhaps $210 billion worth of goods and services. The second case requires giving up consumer goods now with the promise of more in the future through growth in productive capacity. If people choose not to consume 15 percent of the output produced they presumably do so in the expectation of greater consumption in the future. In the example, if $30 billion worth of goods is willingly not consumed in the present period, then the investment of $30 billion is at least as desirable to consumers as the equivalent value of consumer goods. For this reason, any net increase in the stock of buildings and equipment is included as part of the measure of production for consumers.

In the case of durable capital goods, it is never certain exactly how much has been used up during the accounting period. The expenditures for new equipment and buildings can be obtained with greater reliability than the value of capital goods used up. Consequently, a distinction is made between *gross investment*, the purchases of all new buildings and equipment plus additions to business inventories, and *net investment*, the same purchases minus an allowance for the value of buildings and equipment used up during the period. This difference between gross investment and net investment is called *capital consumption allowances*.

Another problem in formulating a measure of final product arises because many economic decisions are made by governments. In the U.S. economy all three levels of government — local, state, and federal — exercise substantial control over resources. Police and fire protection, education, highways, missiles, and public parks are only a few examples of the wide range of government purchases. Most such purchases of goods and services are a form of collective consumption. They are purchases for the household sector but financed by assessment (taxes) instead of allowing individuals to determine for themselves how much of these things to buy. It has been decided that there are desired projects that can be more effectively handled through government agencies. For example, how could a person be sold his share of national defense if not by a legally binding assessment? All government purchases of goods and services are treated as collective consumption, that is, as if these are final products for consumers. The practice, however, is to keep government purchases as a separate category in the national income accounts rather than including it in the consumption figure.

The existence of international trade creates still another problem in measuring final product. The items imported from other countries by consumers, businesses, and governments in the U.S. have not been produced in the U.S.; French wines, Swiss watches, and Japanese toys purchased by U.S. residents are in the figure for U.S. consumption expenditures. Since none of these items are part of U.S. production, they do not belong in a measure of net national product. At the same time U.S. goods are being exported to other countries. These goods, produced in the U.S., have not been included in any of the categories of purchases mentioned so far. Therefore, the value of exports should be added into the measure of domestic production while imports should be excluded. Both of these adjustments are accomplished in one step in the national income accounts by adding an item called *net exports*, which is equal to the value of exports minus imports.

Even though positive net exports represent on balance production of goods that go out of the country, this production is still of value to people within the domestic economy. When country A sells more to country B than B sells to A, then country A has increased its claims on the future production of country B. These claims are similar to putting aside current production in the form of additions to the stock of investment goods. More can be made available in the future because of this current production not immediately consumed. If a country imports more than it exports, it adds to its debt to (or reduces its claims on) foreign countries and must devote a portion of future output to paying off any foreign debt when the debt is eventually due to be paid off. That case is similar in effect to running down the country's stock of investment goods.

Net national product equals the sum of consumption, net investment, government purchases of goods and services, and net exports. In a consumer-oriented economy, the ultimate user is the consumer, but production not consumed has been treated as if it were at least as valuable to the consumer as the goods he does receive.

Gross national product (GNP) is the sum of consumption, *gross* investment, government purchases, and net exports. GNP does include some intermediate products (buildings and equipment used up) and hence involves some double counting. It is less than an ideal measure, but since it is easier than NNP to obtain, GNP is often cited as the measure of the economy's productiveness. Furthermore, one drawback to reported figures for NNP is the uncertainty about what constitutes a precise measure of capital consumption. The usual practice is to let capital consumption allowances equal depreciation charges by businesses. Such depreciation charges, however, are often determined by what is allowable for tax purposes rather than established to reflect as accurately as possible the decline in value of capital goods.[2]

2   U.S. NATIONAL INCOME AND PRODUCT ACCOUNTS

Table 4.1 presents the national income and product accounts for the U.S. economy in 1967. The fact that the report covers a period of time, in this case a year, indicates that the entries in the table are flows. There are two sides to the table. The right side is called the *product side*. To the left is the *allocations side*. The reasons for these designations will become apparent in the discussion of the items contained in the table.

The product side lists the same categories discussed in the preceding section. A look at the accompanying numbers gives an idea of the relative magnitudes in the U.S. of the items that go into this figure called gross national product. Consumption accounts for about 62 percent of the total GNP of $789.7 billion in 1967, and government purchases of goods and services for about 23 percent. Gross investment, labeled Gross Private Domestic Investment has been split into two categories. *Fixed investment* means the total production of new buildings and equipment. *Change in business inventories* is the addition to the stock of unsold inventories held by the business sector. *Net exports*, the difference between exports and imports, for the U.S. come to less than one percent of the GNP. NNP is found to be $720.5 billion by subtracting the measure of capital consumption of $69.2 billion, found on the left side of Table 4.1, from the GNP figure.

People receive payment for their services in producing NNP. In fact, the total value of the services rendered in producing an output is precisely equal to the value of that output. This must be true since profits in any income statement are always defined as the difference between revenues and current costs. It follows that every part of NNP can be allocated to some recipient of income. How it follows will be demonstrated in Sections 3–5 below. For now it is sufficient to note that adding up all of the allocations is another way of obtaining a measure of the total value of goods and services produced. The categories into which GNP is allocated are shown on the left side of Table 4.1.

---

[2]The more a business can charge as a depreciation expense, the smaller its before-tax profits and hence the smaller the tax liability. The Internal Revenue Service allows businesses to choose among alternative depreciation schemes. Many businesses prefer the fastest allowable rate of depreciation in order to defer to the future as much of their tax obligations as possible. When the law changes and businesses change their depreciation rates, capital consumption may appear to change when in fact there is no significant difference in the rate at which investment goods are used up in production, only a difference in the depreciation charges recorded on the books.

Table 4.1   National Income and Product Accounts, U.S. Economy, 1967,
(in billions of dollars)

Allocation Side		*Product Side*		
Compensation of employees	468.2	Personal consumption expenditures		492.2
Proprietors' income	60.7	Gross private domestic investment		114.3
Rental income of persons	20.3	Fixed investment	108.2	
Corporate profits	80.4	Change in business inventories	6.1	
Net interest	23.3	Net exports of goods and services		4.8
NATIONAL INCOME	652.9	Government purchases of goods and services		178.4
Indirect business taxes	69.6			
Capital consumption allowances	69.2			
Statistical discrepancy and other adjustments	−2.0			
GROSS NATIONAL PRODUCT	789.7	GROSS NATIONAL PRODUCT		789.7

Source: *Survey of Current Business*, July 1968.

For the economy as a whole, the portion of net national product that is not consumed becomes an addition to the stock of investment goods.[3] As noted in Chapter 2, the business sector obtains funds necessary to purchase investment goods by selling bonds and stock certificates. The return to individuals who own these securities is partly interest on bonds (or loans) and partly profits to the stockholders of the firms. Both interest and profits, therefore, represent payments for the services of investment goods, just as wages are payments for labor services. Thus, payments for services rendered in producing the final product should fall into one of three categories: wages and salaries, interest, and profits.

Compensation of employees in Table 4.1 covers wages and salaries. It includes all social security contributions and personal income taxes so that the total represents what businesses have had to pay for the services of labor, even if the workers never see part of the payments.

Except for some minor adjustments for foreign transactions, *net interest* is interest paid by the business sector less interest received by the business sector. Thus, the "net" refers to payment of interest on funds borrowed from outside of the business sector.

Corporate profits are defined as revenues less current costs of incorporated

[3]This stock is also frequently called *capital stock*.

enterprises. A finer breakdown of this category separates corporate profits into three parts: corporate profits taxes, dividends, and retained earnings.

Table 4.1 lists other items the names of which do not make clear whether they can be classified as wages, interest, or profits. It turns out that two of these items can be so classified.

Proprietors' income is a mixture of wages and profits. A man in business for himself, or in a partnership, will have earnings that include both the salaries of the owners and the profits on their financial investment in the business. Rather than try to sort out the wage and profit components of earnings from nonincorporated businesses, the national income accountants have a separate category called proprietors' income.

Rental Income of Persons arises because so many people own the houses in which they live. If a family rents from a landlord, the profits that the owner makes (after allowing for depreciation, interest, and other expenses connected with maintaining the building) goes into corporate profits if the owner is a corporation or else into proprietors' income. Owner-occupied houses are treated in the same manner. The national income accountants pretend that the owner pays himself a rent, which is included in the consumption figure in the accounts. This imputed rent, as it is called, is based on going rents on comparable property and is allocated to various categories of expenses in the same manner as any business income. The profit that remains after these other allocations is the item called rental income of persons. The figure of over $20 billion in 1967 indicates that this is not a trivial adjustment in the U.S. accounts.

The total of these five items — compensation of employees, proprietors' income, rental income of persons, corporate profits, and net interest — is a measure of all payments of wages and salaries, interest, and profits. It is called *national income*, a counterpart to the concept of net national product. NNP measures the value of final goods and services produced during a period of time. National income measures the payments for services of labor and investment goods used in producing the final products. National income in the U.S. in 1967 came to $652.9 billion while NNP was much larger, $720.5 billion. This discrepancy is primarily attributable to the existence of indirect business taxes in the U.S. economy.

Indirect business taxes include sales, excise and property taxes. On the one hand, these taxes are included in the market prices of the final products, and market prices provide the yardstick by which different products are added together into a single total. On the other hand, these taxes do not represent payments either for labor services or for services of investment goods, and hence do not belong in national income. They could be treated as payments for services rendered to business by governments for such things as police and fire protection, roads, and sewer systems, but these taxes are generally not earmarked for such purposes. The solution has been to show indirect business taxes in the national income accounts as a separate entry that is the primary cause of the observed discrepancy between national income and NNP.

With the addition of indirect business taxes and capital consumption allowances to national income, the resulting total is another measure of GNP. In theory, the two sides of the accounts should show exactly the same totals. In practice they differ because the estimates on the two sides of the accounts are often assembled from different sources which do not exactly match the theoretical specifications of the accountants. Therefore an entry called *statistical discrepancy* shows the extent to which the two approaches give different estimates. A few relatively minor adjustments, not discussed here, have been included in Table 4.1 with the figure for statistical discrepancy.

3 DISPOSABLE INCOME AND REAL NNP

Two other concepts within the U.S. national income accounts bear noting. One is called disposable personal income or more frequently just *disposable income*. This is the income that people have available to spend or save as they choose after meeting their income tax obligations. The importance of the concept arises from a much used hypothesis about consumer behavior. It is believed that the amount people spend for consumer goods is influenced primarily by the amount of their disposable income.

National income measures the costs associated with the use of the services of labor and investment goods. Not all of these costs to business are actually received by the household sector. Income taxes withheld, social security contributions and private pension plans are part of the cost to businesses of using labor, but they are not paid to individuals during the accounting period. Furthermore only those profits of a business that are paid to the owners should be included in disposable income. Corporate profits taxes and retained earnings are not paid to the owners during the accounting period and so are not part of disposable income.

While income taxes and retained earnings are in national income and not in disposable income, there are some items that are in disposable income but not in national income. These are called *transfer payments*, defined as payments for which no services are performed in return. Since national income is the measure of the total value of direct services, transfer payments evidently do not belong in national income; but transfer payments are received by people and so should be counted as part of disposable income. The great bulk of the transfer payments come from government: unemployment compensation, social security retirement benefits, welfare payments, and veterans' benefits are cases of transfer payments. Another major item included as a transfer payment is interest on government debt. One reason is that these payments, unlike payments of interest by business, cannot be associated directly with the services of investment goods. In any event, transfer payments do add to people's disposable income. These adjustments are shown in Table 4.2 for the U.S. economy for 1967.

Table 4.2   Relationship between National Income and Disposable Income; U.S. Economy, 1967 (in billions of dollars)

National Income			652.9
Add:	Transfer payments		75.3
			728.2
Less:	Personal taxes	82.5	
	Contributions for social insurance	41.9	
	Corporate profits taxes and retained earnings	57.5	181.9
Disposable Personal Income			546.3

Another important concept is *real* net national product. Net national product was $720.5 billion in the U.S. in 1967. In 1958, net national product was $408.4 billion. By comparison, the figure of $720.5 billion for 1967 is 76 percent higher than the figure of $408.4 billion for 1958. Does this mean that the economy's production of final goods and services has grown by 76 percent in just nine years?

If there were no price changes over these years then clearly we could say that aggregate output grew by that amount. However, if prices on the average had gone up by 76 percent, then the 1967 figure would not represent any real increase at all over 1958. Roughly the same volume of goods and services would just be 76 percent more expensive. As a matter of fact, prices did rise somewhat. According to the national income accountants, prices rose approximately 17.3 percent from 1958 to 1967. This means that, given all the items included in net national product, it took about $11.73 in 1967 to buy what could have been purchased for $10 in 1958.

To find out what the 1967 net national product is worth in terms of 1958 dollars, divide $720.5 billion by 1.173. The result: $614.2 billion. This can be interpreted as follows: $720.5 billion in 1967 could buy as much as $614.2 billion could have bought in 1958. Therefore, the figure of $614.2 billion is called *1967 net national product in 1958 prices*, or *1967 net national product in constant (1958) dollars*. The adjustments for changes in purchasing power of the dollar makes it possible to compare the 1958 net national product figure with the adjusted 1967 figure to see how much growth there was in real terms. Since 614.2 is slightly more than 50 percent higher than 408.4, we say there was an increase in *real net national product* of about 50 percent.

This adjustment for the U.S. economy is made in order to eliminate the effects of price changes and to see what the changes over time have been in terms of the quantities of actual goods and services provided. The aim is to compare output at two different times in some sort of common physical unit.

The student interested in the wealth of available data about the U.S. economy should consult the *Survey of Current Business*, a monthly publication of the Office of Business Economics in the U.S. Department of Commerce. Preliminary estimates of the national income accounts are published on a quarterly basis, and each July issue contains the official accounts for the preceding year. Periodic supplements to the *Survey of Current Business* discuss the underlying rationale, sources, and methods for compiling the accounts.

4   VALUE ADDED

The remaining pages of this chapter develop the "classroom income accounts," which are to the classroom economy what the national income accounts are to the U.S. economy: a summary report on the overall level of productive activity within the economy. In this development, the link between the income statements of individual firms and the accounts for the entire economy can be specified more readily, because the accounts of the classroom firms are simpler than those of U.S. businesses.

The data in Table 3.2 in the preceding chapter will be used to show how an income statement can be manipulated into a form that shows a firm's contributions to national income and NNP.

The firm sells $19,000 to consumers during month 1. It also adds $1800 to its inventories. This suggests that the firm is responsible for a total contribution of $20,800 toward final product. The figures in Table 4.3, part A, taken directly from Table 3.2, show how this $20,800 is allocated to costs of materials, labor, interest, profits, and depreciation. Labor costs are recorded as wages, and the interest payments on short-term and long-term debt are both in interest. Profits in Table 4.3 refer to net earnings in the earlier table. By the very manner in which net earnings are computed, it must be true that sales plus changes in inventories will always equal the sum of these allocations.

Not all of this $20,800 value of final goods has actually been created by this firm. The materials, in particular, were produced by another manu-

Table 4.3   A Producer of Consumer Goods Products and Allocations Illustrative Month 1

			Part A	
Allocations			*Products*	
Materials	$ 8,500		Sales to Consumers	$19,000
Wages	8,500		Change in Inventories	1,800
Interest	1,650			
Depreciation	1,200			$20,800
Profits	950			
	$20,800			

		Part B		
Allocations		*Products*		
Wages	$ 8,500	Sales to Consumers		$19,000
Interest	1,650	Change in Inventories		1,800
Profits	950			
				$20,800
Net Value Added	$11,100	Less: Materials		8,500
Depreciation	1,200			
		Contribution to GNP		$12,300
Gross Value Added	$12,300			

NOTE: Data in this table came originally from Table 3.2.

facturer. The firm has taken $8500 worth of materials and transformed them into new items worth $20,800 by utilizing the services of its labor, equipment, and managerial talent. Any increment in value made possible by the services of a firm is known as *value added*.

Because of the distinction between gross national product and net national product, it is necessary to distinguish also between gross and net value added by the firm. The gross value added by the firm in the example is $13,300, which equals $20,800 minus the purchases of intermediate products worth $8500. The $13,300 is allocated to wages, interest, profits, and depreciation. The equipment, however, was originally produced by another firm. The depreciation allocation of $1200 is technically for the purchase of an intermediate product, that is, equipment used up. Subtracting $1200 from $13,300 leaves a figure of $11,100, which represents the firm's contribution to net national product, also called its *net value added*.

Part B of Table 4.3 shows these manipulations. The absence of indirect business taxes and statistical discrepancies in the classroom economy allows national income and net national product to coincide. The net value added of the firm in the example is also its contribution to national income. These manipulations of the firm's income statement should also make clear why a measure of gross product can be obtained in one of two ways. The first way is to add the firm's sales and changes in inventories and then subtract its purchases from other firms. The other way is to add up all of its allocations to wages, interest, profits, and (in the case of gross value added) to depreciation.

5 ADDITIONAL FINANCIAL DATA FOR THE CLASSROOM ECONOMY

More financial information is needed about producers of equipment and of materials in order to derive the aggregate accounts for the classroom economy. These two industries need not be discussed in detail since all of the key decisions are made by managers of firms producing consumer goods. Only information relevant to the construction of the aggregate accounts is provided here. Throughout this section and the next section, it is assumed that there are exactly 10 firms producing consumer goods in the classroom economy.[4]

Producers of equipment have $1,200,000 worth of equipment to be used in the production of more equipment. Since equipment deteriorates at a rate of .5 percent per month, these producers will need to supply themselves with $6000 worth or 5 units of equipment per month in order to maintain their own productive capacity. According to the rules specified in Chapter 3 each producer of consumer goods requires 1 unit or $1200 worth of equipment each month. Ten such firms therefore demand $12,000 worth of equipment every month. Manufacturers of materials also order $12,000 worth of equipment every month. Total monthly sales of $30,000 are shown on the right side of Table 4.4.

In order to meet this demand, these producers need $8000 worth of materials and $4000 worth of labor. Depreciation charges are $6000, and

Table 4.4 Producers of Equipment Monthly Sales and Allocations Illustrative Month 1

Materials	$ 8,000	Sales to Producers:	
Labor Costs	4,000	of consumer goods	$12,000
Interest	5,000	of equipment	6,000
Depreciation	6,000	of materials	12,000
Profits	7,000		
Total Allocations	$30,000	Total Sales	$30,000

[4]If the teacher decides to have 20 firms, all figures in the accounts should be doubled. In fact, any number of firms can be used and the figures adjusted by the ratio of the number of firms to the 10 assumed here.

there is a debt that requires $5000 per month in interest payments. These costs total $23,000, leaving a monthly profit of $7000. These allocations are shown on the left side of Table 4.4.

From the discussion of value added, it should be apparent that the producers of equipment have a gross value added of $22,000 (contribution to GNP) and a net value added of $16,000 (contribution to NNP).

Producers of materials own 2000 units of equipment worth $2,400,000. Their level of production can vary from month to month. It depends on the size of the incoming orders from the producers of consumer goods plus the standing order of $8000 worth of materials from the producers of equipment. Their major cost is for labor services. Every $100 worth of materials produced requires $50 worth of labor. They also pay a total of $12,000 per month in salaries (included in labor cost). Twelve thousand dollars worth of equipment wears out each month, and so their depreciation charges are $12,000. As assumed for other firms in the economy, the equipment that wears out is automatically replaced. These producers' debt requires monthly interest payments of $8000. For simplicity assume that no materials are needed in the production of materials.

The foregoing information enables one to show the product and allocations side of the accounts for producers of materials, once the size of their new orders is known. In the example that underlies Tables 3.2 and 4.3 each producer of consumer goods orders $8500 worth of materials. With ten orders of $8500, sales of materials to producers of consumer goods total $85,000; and total sales, as shown in Table 4.5, are $93,000. On the

Table 4.5 Producers of Materials Sales and Allocations Illustrative Month 1

Labor Costs	$58,500	Sales to Producers:	
Interest	8,000	of consumer goods	$85,000
Depreciation	12,000	of equipment	8,000
Profits	14,500		
		Total Sales	$93,000
Total Allocations	$93,000		

allocations side, the labor costs of $58,500 are $46,500 (50 percent of $93,000) plus $12,000 for salaries. Gross value added by these producers is always equal to the value of their sales. Net value added will always equal sales minus the depreciation allowance of $12,000.

6 THE CLASSROOM INCOME ACCOUNTS

Once the firms' income statements have been manipulated as indicated above, the aggregates can be obtained in a straightforward manner. Table

4.6, called the Classroom Income and Product Table, has been prepared in a manner similar to the U.S. Income and Product Accounts shown in Table 4.1. The numbers in Table 4.6 are taken directly from the financial accounts of the firms in the classroom economy for illustrative month 1.

Net exports will always be zero in the classroom economy. A fuller treatment of macroeconomic adjustments should take into account international trade, but many of the principles and much of the analytical approach to be developed here can be carried over to an analysis of an open economy, that is, an economy with international trade.

Government is also shown with a zero in Table 4.6. The potential impact

Table 4.6   Classroom Income and Product Table Illustrative Month 1

Wages	$147,500	Consumption	$190,000
Interest	29,500	Gross Investment	
Profits	31,000	Equipment	30,000
		Inventory Change	18,000
National Income	$208,000	Government	0
Capital Consumption	30,000	Net Exports	0
GNP	$238,000	GNP	$238,000

on the classroom economy from possible government spending and taxing decisions will be considered later. It may be supposed that some of the purchases now classified as consumption are actually purchases by government. This complication, however, will be deferred to Chapter 8.

The figure for consumption is taken directly from the information presented in Table 4.3 for a single producer of consumer goods. Since each of ten firms has sold $19,000 worth of goods to consumers, consumption totals $190,000.

Gross investment in the classroom economy consists of two components: new equipment and change in inventories. The sales of new equipment, shown in Table 4.5, are $30,000. Inventory changes are incurred only by the producers of consumer goods. Each firm in the example has increased inventories by $1800. If ten firms have had the same increase, the recorded change in inventories is $18,000. The figures on the product side of the account are therefore easy to obtain from the preceding information. GNP is $238,000.

The income side is almost as easily obtained from Tables 4.3, 4.4, and 4.5. The figure for wages of $147,500 in Table 4.6 is the sum of payments to labor of $95,000 (10 × $9500), $4000, and $58,500 in Tables 4.3–4.5. The interest, profits, and capital consumption figures are obtained by the same summation operation.

If each of the ten firms producing consumer goods has a different income statement, the national income and product account can still be obtained by summing the individual firms' allocations to wages, interest, profits, depreciation, their sales, and their change in inventories. If all the data are complete for all firms the two sides must balance because the individual accounts are taken from income statements with profits defined as an allocation that makes the accounts balance.

Once the classroom economy has been in operation, official classroom income accounts can be supplied by the teacher. Since gross investment in equipment and capital consumption will always be equal to $30,000 in every period, it is convenient to omit these items and present the data in the simpler format of Table 4.7. Entries for government purchases and net exports have also been eliminated. Finally, interest and profits have been combined, since analysis of the classroom economy will not require that they be separated.

Providing official reports in terms of dollars may be more confusing than helpful. The managers of individual firms are going to report their orders of materials and plans for production in terms of physical units. Demand (potential sales) will be announced to the firms as a number of units of consumer goods that the household sector wishes to purchase. It will be convenient therefore to express the classroom income accounts in the same units used for these basic decisions. One unit of consumer goods always sells for $250. Any dollar figure (such as $1000) divided by $250 gives the number of units of consumer goods that those dollars can purchase (4 in the case of $1000). The entries in Table 4.7 are obtained

Table 4.7   Classroom Income Accounts Illustrative Month 1 Figures in Real Terms (in units of consumer goods)

Wages	590.0	Consumption	760.0
Interest and Profits	242.0	Inventory Change	72.0
National Income	832.0	Net National Product	832.0

by dividing the corresponding dollar figures in Table 4.6 by $250. The figure of 832 for net national product, for example, is equivalent to $208,000, in that $208,000 can purchase 832 units of consumer goods at $250 per unit.

This operation is analogous to the process of deflating for price changes in the computation of *real net national product* for the U.S. economy. The entries in Table 4.7 are in *real terms*, that is, they are expressed as an equivalent to a number of consumer goods. Any arbitrary unit could be used. Units of consumer goods have been chosen to coincide with the basic decision variables and to simplify the later analysis of the possible dynamic processes at work in the classroom economy.

This completes the discussion of the national income accounts and the classroom income accounts. Since understanding usually comes from experience with material, the class will be asked in subsequent chapters to make use of the data generated by its own classroom economy as reported in the official classroom income accounts.

To appreciate more fully the manipulations performed on the income statement of firms in the classroom economy, the students should perform the following *suggested exercise:* Find an income statement for any company (perhaps in an annual report). Then combine and manipulate the items into a form that shows clearly the company's contribution to national income and net national product.

5

THE THEORY OF INCOME DETERMINATION

In real terms, NNP increased by 50 percent from 1958 to 1967. Why? Why was NNP the size it was in 1958 or in 1967? An analytical approach to why NNP is of a particular magnitude over a period of time is known as *the theory of income determination*. This chapter explains the theory in one of its simplest forms and introduces such key concepts as aggregate demand, the consumption function, and the multiplier. Chapters 7, 8, and 9 introduce slightly more complex versions.

The theory is a formalized interpretation of some of the ideas presented by J. M. Keynes in a book known as *The General Theory*.[1] At the heart of various formulations of this theory, developed by economists in the decades since the publication of Keynes' book, is the notion that the level of economic activity depends on aggregate demand. Hypotheses about what determines aggregate demand in turn rest upon assumptions about what influences the spending decisions of the household and business sectors.

In the classroom economy, similar assumptions will be made about consumer behavior. The students as managers will have a chance to observe their own behavior and to see how the theory can be used to explain the level of NNP. The last three sections of this chapter describe what the students must do to manage firms, and the appendix provides instructions for the teacher to get the economy into operation.

---

[1]The full reference is: John Maynard Keynes, *The General Theory of Employment, Interest and Money* (London: Macmillian and Co., Ltd., 1936).

1   THE CONSUMPTION FUNCTION

Aggregate demand is the combined demand by consumers, businesses, and governments for final goods and services. In other words, it is the total quantity of final products that people, in all sectors of the economy, are planning to buy during a period of time. The theory of income determination is most readily grasped for the first time in its simplest form. Therefore, for the moment, we neglect government demand. We also assume that businesses have no plans to change their stock of investment goods. In this case, aggregate demand consists only of demand for goods and services by the household sector. The theory will be developed in this chapter on the basis of that assumption.

Many economists have studied consumer behavior. There is no certainty about how much consumers are going to spend in any period of time. There are, however, a number of hypotheses about what influences consumers' spending decisions. Students should consider what they think influences their own spending and that of people they know. Are these influences likely to be widespread and systematic throughout the economy? This is the approach Keynes took in *The General Theory.* He postulated factors that he felt could influence consumer spending and considered how important each was likely to be. His conclusion was that, while a number of factors may exert some influence, the primary determinant is what we now call disposable income. In fact he asserted what he called a "fundamental psychological law"[2] that "men are disposed, as a rule and on the average, to increase their consumption as their income increases, but not by as much as the increase in their income."

Keynes' assertion is an example of an assumed behavioral relationship. Whether or not it is true is another matter. It should be treated as an hypothesis to be tested against observed consumer behavior. In the last section of Chapter 6 such an exercise is suggested for the class. Students will be asked to form their own judgments on the basis of data from the U.S. economy. Even though the relationship does not hold exactly, most economists are willing to accept the hypothesis provisionally, that is, they are willing to accept it until evidence accumulates to the contrary or another hypothesis has even stronger evidence in its favor.

Suppose then that there is an economy with no government demand and one in which businesses have no plans to change their stock of investment goods. With the assumed absence of governments, there are no taxes or government transfer payments to consider. If, in addition, all business profits are paid out as dividends, then disposable income,

[2]Keynes, *Op. cit.,* p. 96.

national income, and net national product are all equal. We shall specify a simple "consumption function" for such an economy.

The simplest kind of formula, or functional relationship, that can link consumer spending to income is a straight line.[3] We represent our variables symbolically:

$$C = \text{consumption expenditures (in dollars per period)}$$

$$Y = \text{net national product (in dollars per period)}$$

Now suppose that consumer behavior can be characterized by the following equation:

$$C = 200 + 0.75Y \tag{5.1}$$

Equation (5.1) is called a *consumption function*, since it shows consumption as a function of some other variable or variables. In this case the only

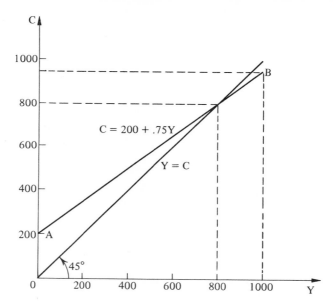

Figure 5.1   An Illustrative Consumption Function and the
Corresponding Stationary State at Y = 800

independent variable (that is, the only variable affecting consumption) in the consumption function is Y. Given the level of Y there is a predictable level of consumption C as long as consumers make their spending decisions

[3]Even if the function is believed to be more complicated, it is convenient to use a straight-line approximation to the function over some range of values of disposable income.

in accordance with this functional relationship. For example, if $Y = 1000$, then:

$$C = 200 + .750 (1000) = 200 + 750 = 950.$$

Point B in Figure 5.1 represents the pair of values $Y = 1000$ and $C = 950$. Since equation (5.1) is the equation for a straight line only one more point is needed to draw this consumption function. The easiest point to find is the C-intercept. When $Y = 0$, the value for C is 200. The point $Y = 0$, $C = 200$ is labeled A in Figure 5.1. The straight line through the points A and B represents the consumption function of equation (5.1).

The marginal propensity to consume (frequently abbreviated to *MPC*) is defined as the ratio, along the consumption function, of a change in consumption to a change in income. With consumption function (5.1), if income is 1000 then consumption will be 950. If income is 1100 then consumption will be 1025. Neither of these levels may ever be observed unless income happens to be 1000 or 1100, but if income were to change by 100 from 1000 to 1100, consumption would rise by 75 from 950 to 1025. The ratio of this change in consumption of 75 to the change in income of 100 equals .75 or ¾. The value of the marginal propensity to consume is therefore .75 in this example. Note that when the consumption function is a straight line (that is, when it is linear), the slope of the line is the same between any two points. Therefore, the coefficient of income (.75 in the example) in a linear consumption function is the value of the MPC.

Keynes' "fundamental psychological law" can be interpreted in terms of the MPC. The first part of the quotation, to the effect that consumption increases as income increases, says that the MPC will be positive. The second part, that consumption will not increase by as much as income, means that the MPC will be less than one. Equation (5.1) clearly satisfies these conditions since .75 is positive and less than one.

One other bit of notation will be introduced here. The symbol Δ will always·mean "change" or "a change in." For example, ΔC means a change in consumption and ΔY means a change in NNP. With these symbols, one can write:

$$MPC = \frac{\Delta C}{\Delta Y}$$

This is a shorthand expression for the definition of the marginal propensity to consume.

2 THE STATIONARY STATE

In Chapter 2, a stationary state was described as a state of affairs that repeats itself period after period with no tendencies for anything to change. Given that consumers' plans to buy consumer goods can be described by the consumption function of equation (5.1), is there some level of NNP at which two conditions are met: consumption is compatible with the consumption function (consumer intentions are carried out) and businesses can keep their stock of investment goods constant (as they had intended)? If so, that level of NNP could continue until either consumers or businesses change their plans.

Aggregate supply is the total production of final goods and services. At first this may seem like unnecessary terminological baggage, for it gives NNP another name. The term aggregate supply has been introduced to emphasize the fact that production decisions are not made by the same people who make purchasing decisions. There is no reason why the quantity of consumer goods produced by businesses must necessarily be equal to the quantity of goods consumers intend to purchase. The two quantities may be equal, and there are likely to be forces bringing them into equality, but they do not have to be equal. After all, businessmen do make mistakes, sometimes bringing out unsuccessful products and at other times seriously underestimating the demand for a product.

A requirement for the stationary state is that aggregate supply equal aggregate demand. Otherwise, something can be expected to change. For example, if demand exceeds the supply of goods produced, then either some buyers cannot obtain what they were planning to buy or else businesses must sell items out of inventories. In the former case, buyers' plans are frustrated. In the latter case, businesses are unable to carry out their plans to have no change in the stock of investment goods. In either case, production will likely increase in the subsequent period. Conversely, when aggregate supply exceeds aggregate demand, production exceeds purchases and producers find themselves with unwanted additions to inventories.

Therefore, an *equilibrium condition,* a condition that must be met in order to maintain the stationary state, is:

$$\text{aggregate supply} = \text{aggregate demand} \qquad (5.2)$$

Aggregate supply, which is equal to net national product, can be denoted by Y. If aggregate demand consists only of consumer demand, then aggregate demand can be denoted by C. In this simple case the equilibrium condition becomes:

$$Y = C \qquad (5.3)$$

Since consumption C has been assumed to be a function of Y, it is possible to substitute for C in equation (5.3) and find the level of net national product at which aggregate supply and demand will be equal. Assume that the consumption function is the one presented in equation (5.1). Substituting the right side of equation (5.1) for C in equation (5.3) gives:

$$Y = 200 + .75\,Y$$

This is now a single equation in the one unknown Y. By a few algebraic manipulations it is possible to solve explicitly for Y:

$$Y - .75Y = 200$$

$$.25Y = 200$$

$$Y = 200/.25 = 800$$

This solution provides the following information and nothing more: If consumers behave in accordance with the consumption function (5.1) and if aggregate supply equals consumer demand, then net national product will equal 800. It is convenient to denote the equilibrium level by a symbol that sets it apart from the actual level since equilibrium may or may not be achieved. A bar over the Y serves this purpose. Thus, $\bar{Y}$ denotes the equilibrium level of net national product. In the example, $\bar{Y} = 800$. At an income of 800, consumers will buy all of the product and save nothing. This is the nature of a stationary state. All of the final product is consumed so that there is no change in the stock of capital goods or in the productive capacity of the economy.

This same solution is shown in Figure 5.1, in which there is a line that corresponds to the equilibrium condition (5.3) as well as a line already discussed for the consumption function (5.1). The line labeled $Y = C$ is known as the 45° line. In plane geometry, a right angle has 90 degrees. Thus a line that bisects a right angle forms a 45° angle with either one of the sides. The line $Y = C$ will make a 45° angle with one of the axes if there is the same scale along the vertical axis as on the horizontal axis. Each point on this line is the same number of units up from the horizontal axis as it is across from the vertical axis. Now look for the point which satisfies both the equilibrium condition and the consumption function, the point at which the two lines cross. This occurs where $Y = 800$.

For reasons that will become apparent in Chapter 7, this concept of a stationary state will also be called the *long-run equilibrium*.

Whether or not such an equilibrium is stable (see Chapter 2, Section 5) is another question. If net national product is below equilibrium, will it rise toward equilibrium? If it is above equilibrium, will net national product fall? The operation and analysis of the classroom economy should lead the class to answer yes to both of these questions, but the yes may carry some reservations.

3 THE MULTIPLIER

The equilibrium level of NNP depends directly on the nature of the consumption function. Equation (5.1) is one example of a consumption function. Suppose the numbers had been different. How would a change in the numbers change the equilibrium NNP? To answer this question, assume a general linear consumption function:

$$C = A + bY \tag{5.4}$$

The letters A and b in equation (5.4) are called *parameters*. They stand for a whole set of numbers that could be inserted into the function. Note that b stands for the marginal propensity to consume. If $A = 200$ and $b = .75$, then equation (5.1) results. If A and b are left unspecified, it is possible to find the equilibrium level of NNP in terms of A and b. The procedure is the same as before. Assume that the equilibrium condition (5.3) holds and substitute for C from equation (5.4):

$$Y = A + bY$$
$$(1 - b)Y = A$$
$$\bar{Y} = A/(1 - b) \tag{5.5}$$

Table 5.1   Stationary State in Terms of Y for Values of A and b with the Consumption Function $C = A + bY$

A \ b	.50	.60	.70	.75	.80	.90
60						600
80						800
100					500	1000
120					600	
140				560	700	
160			533	640	800	
180			600	720	900	
200			667	800	1000	
220		550	733	880		
240		600	800	960		
260		650	867	1040		
280	560	700	933			
300	600	750	1000			
320	640	800				
340	680	850				
360	720	900				
380	760	950				
400	800	1000				
420	840					
440	880					
460	920					
480	960					
500	1000					

The equilibrium level of NNP can be found directly from equation (5.5) if A and b are known. The assumption that the MPC is between zero and one implies that $(1 - b)$ is also a positive fraction. Since negative production is impossible, it follows that the parameter A must also be positive if the equilibrium level of NNP is to be attainable. Table 5.1 has been prepared from equation (5.5) to show how different values of A and b can alter the equilibrium value of Y. This table can also be used to demonstrate a concept known as the multiplier.

The total demand by consumers, by businesses, and by governments for final products has been called *aggregate demand*. The whole relationship between aggregate demand and net national product will be called an *aggregate demand schedule*. In the absence of government demand and any business investment plans, consumption, when plotted as a function of income, is the same thing as an aggregate demand schedule.

Suppose the consumption function is the one used in the preceding section with $A = 200$ and $b = .75$. Suppose also that Y has settled into its equilibrium level of 800. What happens if the aggregate demand schedule shifts up by 20, as depicted in Figure 5.2? In other words, what happens when people decide to spend more at each level of income? The consumption function becomes:

$$C = 220 + .75Y$$

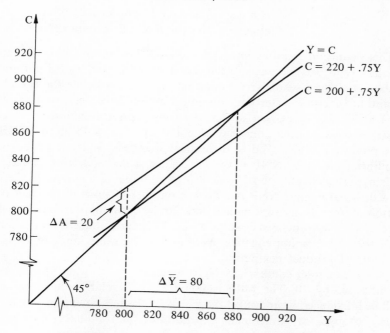

Figure 5.2   An Illustration of a Multiplier Relationship

If this shift in demand were entirely unexpected by producers, they would continue for a while to produce 800 units of consumer goods. The added demand might be met out of available inventories of consumer goods, or, if inventories were low enough, a portion of the demand might go unsatisfied. This is obviously a state of disequilibrium. Once the managers of firms are aware of this increased demand, or if they anticipate it, they will increase their orders of materials and their rate of output of consumer goods.

Suppose production and income rise by 20 units to 820. Will this restore equilibrium? The answer is no. With a positive marginal propensity to consume, consumers will increase spending as income increases. They move along the new consumption schedule. For every unit increase in income, demand increases by three-fourths of a unit. When production and income rise by 20 units, demand rises by 15 units. There is still disequilibrium with consumption in excess of production.

According to the entry in Table 5.1 with $b = .75$ and $A = 220$, equilibrium will not be reestablished until income has reached 880 units. Consider this carefully. An increase of 20 in the aggregate demand schedule increases the equilibrium level of income by 80. There is a four-to-one ratio of the increase in equilibrium income to the initial upward shift in demand. This is an example of the *multiplier*, which is defined as follows:

$$\text{multiplier} = \frac{\text{change in the equilibrium level of NNP}}{\text{change in the value of a flow parameter}}$$

This definition requires an explanation. When the linear consumption function (5.4) was introduced, the terms A and b were called parameters. These stand for a whole set of constants that might define the actual consumption function. After data on consumption have been studied, values of A and b will be chosen so that the consumption function as closely as possible shows actual consumer demand at various levels of NNP. At this point we have asked a theoretical question. What happens to the equilibrium level of NNP if the parameter A changes from 200 to 220? This hypothetical change of 20 in A is an example of a change in the value of a flow parameter. NNP is a flow, a number of units of product over a period of time. Consumption is a flow. In the consumption function, therefore, A must also be measured as a flow in order to have both sides of the consumption function equation measured in the same kinds of units, that is, units of product per period.

In the example, equilibrium NNP increases by 80 when the parameter A increases by 20. The ratio is therefore 4. Similar multiplier concepts will be introduced when we get the effects of changes in business investment plans, changes in government expenditures, and changes in taxes. The value of the multiplier that results from a shift in the consumption function can be determined directly from equation (5.5). Let ΔA denote a change in A and $\Delta \bar{Y}$ denote the corresponding change in $\bar{Y}$. Then from (5.5):

$$\bar{Y} + \Delta \bar{Y} = \frac{A + \Delta A}{1 - b} = \frac{A}{1 - b} + \frac{\Delta A}{1 - b}$$

$$= \bar{Y} + \frac{\Delta A}{1 - b}$$

Therefore $\quad \Delta \bar{Y} = \Delta A/(1 - b)$

or $\quad\quad \dfrac{\Delta \bar{Y}}{\Delta A} = \dfrac{1}{1 - b}$ (5.6)

Thus, with $b = .75$, $1 - b = .25$ and the multiplier $\Delta \bar{Y}/\Delta A = 1/(1 - b) = 4$.

Table 5.1 can be used to check this formula (5.6) for a number of different values of b. When $b = .9$ the multiplier equals 10. In the table it can be seen that equilibrium NNP rises by 10 times any increase in A. When $b = 0.5$ the multiplier equals 2 and any change in A is matched by a change in equilibrium NNP that is twice the change in A.

Why is this? Why does the equilibrium level change by some multiple of the change in the aggregate demand schedule? Examples, when generalized, provide the answer. The total production of final goods during a period is the aggregate supply, and the difference between aggregate demand and aggregate supply is called *excess demand*. Equilibrium occurs when excess demand is zero. Now suppose excess demand equals ΔA as indicated in Figure 5.2. Producers have reason to increase production, but for every unit increase in aggregate supply, aggregate demand also grows by b units, and so excess demand goes down by only $1 - b$. Therefore, in order to reduce excess demand by 1 unit, aggregate demand must grow by $1/(1 - b)$ units. This is the multiplier formula.

Perhaps one more illustration will help the student grasp the argument. If $b = .8$, each increase of 1.0 in income lowers excess demand by .2 units. It should then be evident that an increase of $1/.2 = 5$ units of income is required in order to remove 1 unit of excess demand. If still unconvinced, the student should work out some examples of his own.

The *theory of income determination* rests upon the assumption that the economy will tend to its equilibrium level. Thus, with a plausible hypothesis about how income influences aggregate demand and a belief that the economy is always at or close to its equilibrium level, one can say what the level of net national product will be and what changes it will undergo in response to other influences. This can be a useful theory. It will be discussed more fully in Chapters 7 and 8. In the meantime, the classroom economy will begin operations; and Chapter 6 will consider a procedure for discriminating among alternative hypotheses about the consumption function.

4   GETTING THE ECONOMY MOVING

We turn now to procedural matters, to how the classroom economy operates. Students should be assigned or allowed to volunteer to help manage the firms producing consumer goods. The instructor will designate the number of firms in each economy. This section describes the forms that students, as managers of firms, must fill out and the nature of the decisions in terms of consumer behavior in the classroom economy. Section 6 reviews the students' procedures and sets out a few guidelines for making good decisions. The appendix to this chapter suggests procedures for the teacher, who must oversee the operation of the economy.

Table 5.2 is an example of a record form, which can be copied for use as needed. Each manager should keep his own record form. In that way managers of a firm can cross-check the accuracy of their figures. For practice in filling out the forms and as a means of getting the economy started, the teacher will tell everyone what to do in month 1. After that, the managers will be on their own. The following information is necessary to fill out the form for month 1:

Beginning inventory of materials   _____
Beginning inventory of finished goods   _____
Units of consumer goods produced   _____
Quantity of materials ordered   _____
Potential sales   _____
Dividends   _____

The teacher will supply this information to the class. Suggestions appear in the appendix. Each student should take out a Record Form and put a 1 in the first column for month number 1. As he reads the following explanation of the form, the student should fill out the first column using the data supplied by the teacher. Any reference in parenthesis refers to the corresponding row of the record form. For example, (1) refers to line (1): materials available this period.

Lines (1) and (5) can be filled in directly from the information supplied about beginning inventories of materials and finished goods, respectively. See the directions on the record form for obtaining these figures in periods after month 1.

Lines (2) and (4) represent the two decisions that the managers must make each month. This is why they have an asterisk by the number of the lines. The firm may never produce more consumer goods than it has units of materials available at the beginning of the month. Since each unit of consumer goods produced requires one unit of materials, the same number (units produced) should be entered on line (2) and on line (6).

Line (3) is the difference between the number of units of materials available and the number used. Since production may never exceed the amount of materials available, line (3) may never be negative. It may be zero.

Line (4) is the order for materials that will be delivered at the end of the month and be available for next month's production. This order depends on anticipated sales in the next period, the unused stock of materials from this period and the expected stock of unsold inventories of finished goods. For month 1 the teacher will say what to enter in line (4).

Lines (5) and (6) have already been completed. Line (7) is the sum of the entries in (5) and (6). It is the number of units of consumer goods available for sale. It is also the maximum number of units that the firm can sell during the month no matter how much consumers would like to buy.

Line (8) depends on the consumers. An individual firm can have relatively little direct effect on its own sales, but all firms together do determine, through the consumption function, what each firm's sales will be. At this point, the instructor will record the production decisions and materials-ordered decisions of all firms, compute the household sector's income, ascertain how much the consumers intend to buy, and announce a figure called "potential sales." (These steps are spelled out in the appendix to this chapter.) This figure should be entered in (8).

Potential sales represent each firm's share of the market. Every firm has an equal share. With ten firms, potential sales are one-tenth of the total number of units that consumers intend to buy. If a firm has more units available than the potential sales figure, then the number of units sold, line (9), is equal to potential sales. If a firm does not have enough units available it sells what is available and misses the rest of its potential sales. Therefore, line (9) is the lower of line (7), units available for sale, or (8) potential sales.

The next few lines of the record form provide a short-cut method of figuring the profitability of the firm's operations for the month. The rationale for these calculations is given in Chapter 3. The gross profit, line (10), is equal to the number of units sold times $50. The figure of $50 is the difference between the final selling price and the per-unit variable costs of production.

There are also some costs that do not vary directly with the level of sales. The costs of holding units in inventory are based on the cost of borrowing funds to finance the inventory holdings. On line (11) is recorded the holding costs of materials at $1 per unit in inventory at the beginning

Table 5.2   Record Form

Economy No. ——————   *Firm No.* ——————

Period No.

(1) Materials available this period
[(3) + (4) from last period]

*(2) Production: materials used up
[may not exceed (1)]

(3) Unused materials (1) − (2)

*(4) Materials ordered
[see rules for limit]

(5) Finished goods in inventory
[(7) − (9) from last period]

(6) Units of goods produced
[same as (2)]

(7) Units available (5) + (6)

(8) Potential sales									
(9) Units sold [smaller of (7) or (8)]									
(10) Gross profit $50 \times$ (9)									
(11) Holding costs: $1 \times$ (1)									
(12) Holding costs: $2 \times$ (5)									
(13) Fixed costs $2700									
(14) Dividends $10 \times$ (8)									
(15) (11) + (12) + (13) + (14)									
(16) Retained earnings (10) − (15)									
(17) Cumulative retained earnings									

of the period, and on line (12) the costs of finished goods at $2 per unit. Line (13) is for fixed costs of $2700 for depreciation and interest on long-term debt. Dividends are on line (14). The sum of these additional costs plus dividends are recorded on line (15).

A rule for dividends is suggested on the record form, namely that dividends be equal to $10 times Potential Sales. The instructor, however, may choose to follow some other rule or even decide arbitrarily each period what the level of dividends will be. (See the appendix for a discussion of this.) Whatever the level of dividends announced for a period, every firm in the economy must record the same figure.

Line (16) is for retained earnings. For comparative purposes with other firms, retained earnings are cumulated on line (17) from one month to the next. *The firm's objective will be to make the cumulative retained earnings as large as possible and, if it can, larger than that of any other firm.*

On the basis of the information provided for month 1, each student should be able to compute the national income figures for month 1 by referring back to Chapter 4 where necessary. Such an exercise is strongly recommended.

Beginning in month 2 the managers are entirely on their own to make the production and ordering decisions for their firm. The teacher will explain to the class how he plans to organize the decision procedures. In each period of the classroom economy the managers of firms must make their decisions to order materials and to produce an output *before* the potential sales figure is known. Then, after they have learned the potential sales figure, they compute their firm's earnings for the period and turn their attention to the next period.

5   ALTERNATIVE CONSUMPTION FUNCTIONS

The problem of inferring consumer behavior from the data generated by the economy becomes more interesting if there are a number of alternative hypotheses to consider. One hypothesis discussed so far is that consumption is a linear function of disposable income. Two more possibilities will be added. Chapter 6 is devoted to the problem of inferring from the available data which of these functions best describes consumer behavior. There is to be no pretense that these hypotheses exhaust the plausible relationships between disposable income and consumer spending or even represent more than a very small subset of possible determinants of consumption expenditures. They do provide a manageable number of hypotheses that can be used to illustrate how to approach the more general problem of ascertaining a plausible consumption function for an economy.

In the simplest form of the theory of income determination, consumption is assumed to be a function of disposable income. Within the setting of the classroom economy, however, there is a problem of timing. Disposable income includes dividends paid to owners of the firms, but net earnings and hence dividends depend on sales during the period. Therefore, disposable income cannot legitimately be used in a consumption function that determines firm's sales in the same period. Since the classroom economy is a hypothetical world, considerations of convenience may take precedence over logical purity whenever the objectives of having a classroom economy are not thereby jeopardized. To overcome the timing dilemma, the teacher will use a construct called *spendable income*. Let:

Z_t = spendable income in period t of the classroom economy

Spendable income will be assumed to influence consumer spending in the classroom economy just as disposable income has been assumed to influence consumer spending in a real-world economy. How Z_t can be computed is explained in the appendix. As long as the teacher informs the class about the values of spendable income in each period, it does not greatly matter how it has been computed. One of the problems for the students in Chapter 6 will be to determine how spendable income, whatever its value, influences consumer spending in the classroom economy.

There are three hypotheses about the consumption function that are set out below. When data become available from the classroom economy, the students must try to ascertain which of these three types of functions best accounts for observed consumer behavior.

The symbol C_t will stand for consumption expenditures in period t. Thus, C_1 is consumption in month 1, C_2 is the amount in month 2, and so on. If firms do not have available the goods that consumers intend to buy, actual expenditures in some month may be less than consumers were planning to make. Therefore, another symbol will be used to denote *consumer demand*. C_t^* denotes the amount of consumption if consumers are able to buy as much as they plan to buy in month t. The * distinguishes consumer demand from actual consumption, in case they are not equal.

The three hypotheses are:

I. *Consumer demand is a linear function of current spendable income:*
$$C_t^* = A_\mathrm{I} + b_\mathrm{I}Z_t$$

This is similar to the type of consumption function discussed above, and will be called a type-I consumption function. A_I and b_I are parameters as were A and b in equation (5.4). The subscript I has been added to distinguish these parameters from those in the other hypotheses.

II. *Consumer demand is a linear function of last month's spendable income*:
$$C^* = A_\mathrm{II} + b_\mathrm{II}Z_{t-1}$$

This hypothesis suggests that consumers base their spending decisions not on current spendable income, but on spendable income received a month earlier. It will be called a type-II consumption function.

    III.   *Consumer demand is a systematically shifting linear function of current spendable income:*

$$C_t^* = (A_{\text{III}} + Dt) + b_{\text{III}}Z_t$$

This hypothesis requires additional explanation. The term in parentheses is to be treated as the A term in the consumption functions discussed above. The difference is that the value of $(A_{\text{III}} + Dt)$ changes each month. If D were 5, for example, the consumption function would shift up 5 units every month. This systematic upward shift may be the result of factors that influence consumer behavior over time, a topic discussed in Chapter 7. This function will be called a type-III consumption function.

6   DECISION GUIDELINES

There will be a sequence of events in the classroom economy. Several firms are established, with students as managers. Each firm is given an identifying number. For the first month the teacher tells every firm how many units of consumer goods to produce, how many units of materials to order and how many units of consumer goods that the firm can sell. The managers complete their firms' record forms for month 1. On the basis of this information and a guess about future sales, they make decisions for month 2. Each firm must decide on two numbers for month 2, the number of units of goods to produce and the number of units of materials to order. When potential sales are announced for month 2, the managers compute profits and proceed to make decisions for month 3. So the process continues until the classroom economy is discontinued.

For greatest competitive interest, the managers of a firm should try to make cumulative retained earnings (line (17) on the record form) greater than that of any other firm.

There are only two ways that firms' profits can differ. One way is to have different levels of inventories. The lower the level of inventories, the smaller the holding costs incurred and hence the greater the net profits. The other way is for some firms to miss sales. This latter cost is relatively great: $50 per unit of potential sales not actually sold. It is wise to have adequate inventories so that sales are not missed, but not so many that the firm pays excessive and unnecessary inventory holding costs. The skillful manager will try to tread the line between inadequate and excessive inventories.

A firm may produce any quantity of output during a month provided that it does not exceed the number of units of materials available. Any number of units of materials may be ordered, subject to one limitation. The number ordered by a firm may not differ from the order placed in the previous month by more than 20 units. Managers are well advised to keep this restriction in mind when planning ahead. The teacher will organize the economy and see that it gets underway.

APPENDIX TO CHAPTER 5: SUGGESTED PROCEDURES

To help organize a classroom economy, this appendix suggests some guidelines and provides a number of formulas. The teacher, particularly one who has already experimented with a classroom economy, should not feel bound by the procedures outlined here. There are many ways to operate a classroom economy. One way is spelled out primarily for the teacher who has never tried this sort of approach before.

The tasks that the teacher is to perform can conveniently be discussed in four parts: (1) organizing the classroom economy; (2) choosing the consumption function and initial decisions; (3) keeping records and computing potential sales; (4) preparing classroom income accounts. Each of these will be a section heading in this appendix.

7 ORGANIZING THE CLASSROOM ECONOMY

Ten is the recommended number of firms to have producing consumer goods. This is enough so that one firm cannot have much of an effect on the economy but few enough that the computations are not overly time-consuming. It is also the number for which the arithmetic is the easiest in computing potential sales. The firms should be assigned consecutive numbers from 1 to 10. While one student could run his own firm, two or three managers to a firm allow them to discuss the advisability of alternative strategies. More than three managers may become unwieldy.

If a computer is available, most accounting errors can be avoided and time-consuming efforts to keep records can be eliminated. A sample Fortran IV program and a brief description of the corresponding input and output, which can be used for this purpose, appear at the back of this book. While ten is still a convenient number of firms to have, a computer can handle almost any number.

With large classes it is advisable to have more than one economy rather than to increase substantially the number of firms in a single economy. In this regard, there are advantages to having a class large enough to establish several classroom economies. Each can differ systematically from the others in terms of the parameters in or type of consumption function, the initial stock of inventories, or the initial level of production relative to the position of long-run equilibrium. It is then possible to examine the results to see if the experiences of the various economies differ in ways that theory would have predicted. One economy alike in all other respects to another economy could be used to introduce fiscal policy in a manner similar to the exercise suggested near the end of Chapter 8. Some economies might have antitrust laws, and others allow collusion. There are thus learning possibilities for a large class beyond what can be done with a small class. Experience with a classroom economy and questions from students will generally suggest other interesting variations that could be tried.

Suggestions for the information to be provided to the classroom economy for month 1 are found in the next section. Suppose this information has been given to the class, and everyone has filled out his record form for month 1. The students should then be given the time between class meetings so that managers of a firm can get together to decide on their firm's level of production and order of materials for month 2. These decisions can be handed in when the class meets. The teacher himself should then take the time between classes to check out his own computational procedures before announcing potential sales for month 2. Managers may again be given time between classes to ponder their decisions for month 3. It is wise to start slowly since there is usually some initial confusion about what is happening.

At some point, however, it is recommended that one or two hours, not necessarily consecutive, be set aside in order to get through ten to fifteen months in the classroom economy if there are few enough firms to make this feasible. This will facilitate the analysis of consumer behavior discussed in Chapter 6. If such a session is run with several decisions made consecutively, there is a way to expedite matters. Each firm hands in the two basic decisions, units produced and materials ordered, for the current period. The teacher can quickly record the decisions and compute potential sales. If the managers make their decisions for the next month before they compute profits, they can then take the time to compute profits for the last period while the teacher, or an assistant, is utilizing the current decisions. This avoids having the teacher wait for the managers to figure profits and the managers wait while potential sales are being computed.

The teacher may wish to have copies of the record form reproduced or let the students keep their own records. If a computer is used, all that is needed are small slips of paper on which each firm records the production and ordering decisions for that firm for the month. The bookkeeping is prepared by the computer.

The teacher may terminate the classroom economy at any time. It is best to do so without telling the class in advance which is the last period. This avoids "end-play" decisions. About fifteen periods is usually a sufficient number. The economy should be continued longer only if the teacher believes that the learning possibilities for the students are worth the effort necessary to continue.

8 CHOOSING A CONSUMPTION FUNCTION AND INITIAL DECISIONS

In selecting the consumption function, the teacher is confronted not only with three hypotheses (given in Chapter 5, Section 5) but also with choosing values for the parameters. Whether a function of type I or II is chosen makes little difference. With each such function is associated a stationary state. With a type-III function there is no stationary state. The equilibrium level changes every period. The first step in choosing a consumption function is simply to pick one of these three hypotheses.[4]

The next step is to choose a value for the marginal propensity to consume (b_I, b_{II}, or b_{III} depending on the type of function selected). The value of the MPC is probably the most important influence on the behavior of firms in the classroom economy, primarily because the multiplier depends on it. Suppose firms have excess inventories and managers want to work them off. To do so the managers cut orders and production. Income falls. If the MPC is very high, sales will fall almost as much as production and very few inventories will be worked off. If firms are trying to build up inventories, their efforts will likewise be largely thwarted by a high marginal propensity to consume. The violence of the adjustment process depends on the choice of the MPC. Experience suggests that a value around .85 leads to violent adjustments; one around .65 to mild adjustments.

Once the type of function and the MPC have been chosen, the value of the constant term (A_I, A_{II}, or A_{III} and D) will determine the equilibrium level for the economy. The decision about the equilibrium level should be made in conjunction with the decision of where to start the economy. Table 5.1 can be used as a guide in selecting the constant term. If ten firms share the market equally, then each firm's sales in the stationary state will be one-tenth of the entry in the table. For example, suppose .75 were the value of the MPC. If the A-term in the consumption function were 200, then the stationary state would occur at an output of 800 and each of ten firms would sell 80 units in every period once this long-run equilibrium had been achieved.

[4]A type-III function is not advisable unless the instructor or some of the students can make use of a simple multiple regression program to test whether or not the observations indicate a significant D-term.

One of the main reasons for establishing a classroom economy is to let the students develop for themselves an explanation for the experience of their own classroom economy. In many ways it will be fun for the teacher, too, if he is not sure about exactly how the economy is going to adjust. Nevertheless, he should be aware of the break-even point for the individual firm in his selection of a level for the stationary state. The individual firm's net earnings are close to zero with sales around 56.

Furthermore, with dividends of $10 per unit of potential sales, a firm will need sales of at least 70 in order to realize positive retained earnings. Actually the teacher does not have to follow this formula for dividends. He can vary dividends from period to period at his own discretion if he wishes to keep cumulative retained earnings positive for the firms making the most profitable decisions, negative for firms that are doing the worst, and close to zero on the average.

A long-run equilibrium of close to 80 per firm is recommended if either a type-I or type-II function is selected. The values of A and b shown in Table 5.1 are not the only ones that may be used for A_I and b_I or A_{II} and b_{II}. For example, with 10 firms, if $A_I = 226.8$ and $b_I = .72$, then equation (5.5) can be used to show that the long-run equilibrium occurs when NNP equals 810.

If a type-III function is used, it must be remembered that a stationary state is no longer possible. The equilibrium level shifts by D times the multiplier every month. For example, if $b = .75$, the multiplier is 4. If $D = 1$, the equilibrium level shifts up by 4 every month. If $D = 5$, the equilibrium shifts by 20 each period. Table 5.1 can also be used for suggestions of values of A_{III} and D to use with a type-III function. For example, suppose $b_{III} = .75$, $A_{III} = 200$, and $D = 2$. In month $t = 10$, the constant term in a type-III function ($A_{III} + Dt$) equals 220 and the corresponding temporary equilibrium position will occur with total output and sales of 880, or 88 units per firm. This can be seen from the 880 in Table 5.1 when $b = .75$ and $A = 220$.

The capacity constraint of 100 units per month has been set primarily for illustrative purposes for the theoretical discussions in Chapters 7 and 8 of the possibility of inflation and of the difficulties of maintaining an economy at close to full employment. In a run of the classroom economy, this production ceiling could prematurely choke off a boom. As long as the constraint is maintained that orders of materials may change by no more than 20 units per period (or some such limit), there is little need to impose any limitation on production other than the requirement that it not exceed materials available. An attempt by an individual firm to manipulate demand through large changes in production is likely to benefit other firms more than the manipulating firm.

The final decision concerning the classroom economy is what to tell the class about inventories, production, orders, and sales for month 1. With regard to initial inventories, the first few periods are most interesting if the firms start with plenty of inventories. For this reason, 100 units of materials and 25 units of finished goods, used in the balance sheet illustration in Chapter 3, is the recommended starting position. The teacher should feel free, however, to select any level of initial inventories he wishes.

As for production and orders in month 1, the economy can be started in equilibrium, but again it is more interesting to start in a position of disequilibrium and to watch the process of adjustment. For simplicity, the firms can be told to order as many units of materials in month 1 as the number of units of consumer goods they are told to produce. For example, suppose the equilibrium level is 80 units of output per firm. In month 1, each firm might be told to produce 90 units of consumer goods and to order 90 units of materials.

The one other bit of information to get things started in month 1 is the level of *potential sales* (each firm's maximum sales for the period if it has sufficient goods available). This can be determined by means of the consumption function and the first period production and ordering decisions. The method of computing potential sales is explained in the next section.

9 KEEPING RECORDS AND COMPUTING POTENTIAL SALES

The teacher should see that a record is kept of each economy. A suggested form, classroom economy record, is shown on the next page with some illustrative numbers filled in. The teacher may duplicate copies of this form, without the numbers, or may design and make his own forms. One copy is needed for every period the economy is in operation. With a computer, the printout can include a complete record for the teacher as well as for each firm.

The number at the head of each column of the classroom economy record is the same as the number on the corresponding row of the record form. The classroom economy record can be used for quick calculations when a series of decisions is being made within a single session and for completing other details when there is more time. The following discussion suggests how this form can be used.

The most important columns are (2) and (4) since these show every firm's decisions for the month. In a session when a series of decisions is being made, all that the teacher needs are the totals at the bottom of these two columns. In the example, total production comes to 810 units and total materials ordered is 886 units. The designation of the total at the bottom of column (2) as Q_t and the total at the bottom of column (4) as M_t facilitates the algebraic presentation of the necessary computations for deriving potential sales and the classroom income accounts. For reference,

Q_t = quantity of consumer goods produced in month t

M_t = units of materials ordered in month t

Given these two totals, the next problem is to compute *potential sales*. In the absence of a live set of consumers in the classroom economy, consumer demand must be determined by formula. All of the suggested formulas assume that income influences consumer spending. Whether or not the measure of income conforms precisely to what might influence real consumers is not of great importance. The important points are that there be more than one possible formula and that each bears some resemblance to hypotheses that economists formulate to explain consumer demand in a real economy. In Chapter 6, the students are asked to determine which formula has been used. As long as the class is told the value of spendable income each period, there is no need in the classroom economy to have more "realistic" formulas if they complicate the teacher's task. Thus, the measure called spendable income, an approximation to NNP, will be made as simple as possible to compute.

We suggest defining *spendable income* Z_t by the following formula:

$$Z_t = .5\, Q_t + .5\, M_t \tag{5.A.1}$$

A value for spendable income can be readily computed, with formula (5.A.1), by taking half of total production and half of materials ordered. In the example, spendable income is seen to be 848. Assume that the following type-I consumption function is being used:

$$C_t^* = 372 + .6\, Z_t$$

Substituting for $Z_7 = 848$ yields:

$$C_7^* = 372 + .6\,(848) = 372 + 508.8 = 880.8$$

The figure of 880.8 has been recorded for consumer demand. The item in the table called "random term" will be discussed presently. It may be neglected for the moment. Potential sales are determined on the assumption that all firms share equally in the demand by consumers. It is obtained by dividing consumer demand by the number of firms and rounding to the nearest integer. With ten firms this is an easy operation. In the example, potential sales are 88 units. This figure should be reported to the managers of firms so that they can complete their record form for the period and proceed to make production and ordering decisions for the next period.

If hypothesis III is used, it would simplify computations to have handy

Classroom Economy Record

Economy No. ___1___   Month No. ___7___

Firm No.	(1) Mat. Invent.	(2) Units Produced	(3) Unused Mat. (1) − (2)	(4) Materials Ordered	(5) F.G. Invent.	(7) Units Available (1) + (5)	(9) Units Sold	(14) Dividends	(16) Retained Earnings	(17) Cum. Ret. Earn.
1	90	90	0	95	0	90	88	880	730	
2	90	90	0	95	5	95	88	880	720	
3	90	80	10	90	10	90	88	880	710	
4	90	75	15	80	20	95	88	880	690	
5	90	80	10	85	10	90	88	880	710	
6	90	80	10	90	20	100	88	880	690	
7	80	80	0	95	0	80	80	880	340	
8	90	85	5	90	0	85	85	880	580	
9	80	80	0	95	20	100	88	880	700	
10	90	70	20	70	30	100	88	880	670	
TOTALS		810		886			869			
		Q_t		M_t			C_t			

Consumer demand ___880.8___	Z_t, Spendable income ___848.0___	C_t, Consumption ___869.0___
Random term ___	W_t, Wages ___581.2___	I_t, Investment ___−16.8___
Potential sales ___88___	R_t, Interest and profits ___271.0___	Y_t, NNP ___852.2___

a table of constants to be added each period. For example, suppose the consumption function has $A_{III} = 200$, $D = 4$. The table might look like this:

t	$A_{III} + Dt$
1	204
2	208
3	212
4	216
5	220
6	224
7	228
8	232
...	...

Each period, after spendable income is multiplied by b_{III}, the appropriate constant from such a table is added to get consumer demand.

The columns other than (2) and (4) of the classroom economy record represent bookkeeping details that provide checks on the accuracy of the individual firms' records. All computational procedures are the same as they are for filling out the record form. No entry in either column (3) or column (5) may be negative.

The entries in column (9) for consumer purchases may not exceed the number of units available. If enough is available, actual sales equal potential sales. In the example, firms 7 and 8 did not have enough units available and therefore missed sales. In this example, because two firms had "stock-out" positions (that is, they missed sales), actual consumption is below consumer demand. It would make sense to have this unsatisfied demand carry over into the next period, but computational ease and possible strains during periods of expansion militate against such a procedure. It is best to forget about unsatisfied demand.

Column (16) has been filled out to illustrate the difference in earnings that result from different levels of inventories and from missed sales. The calculation of retained earnings is the same as it is for each individual firm: take $50 times units sold and subtract inventory holding costs, fixed costs of $2700, and dividends. A similar procedure can be followed for the totals at the bottom of the table. The resulting earnings figure can be compared with the sum of the individual earnings as a check on the accuracy of profit calculations.

From the data on orders, production, and sales, it is possible to fill out the inventory position for each firm as of the beginning of the next period. The inventories of materials in column (1) equal materials ordered (4) plus unused materials (3) in the previous period. The beginning inventories of finished goods in column (5) equal goods available (7) minus units sold (9) in the previous period. The totals can also be used to check on the accuracy of the calculations.

Since potential sales are figured by rounding to the nearest integer, the total potential sales may not lie exactly on the consumption function. This means that there may be some apparent random deviations attributable to rounding. Nevertheless, with only a few observations the students will soon have a fairly precise estimate of the consumption function being used (after they have read Chapter 6). Those teachers who think that the students already have enough details to cope with should not worry about the following suggestion. Those who wish to make the analysis of consumer behavior into slightly more of a puzzle for the students should plan to introduce an explicit random component into the consumption function. It is strongly recommended that this be done. The rationale is discussed in Chapter 6. A practical consideration is that minor errors can be treated as a random deviation.

One way to randomize the potential sales figure is to consult a table of random numbers and devise a way to select a series of one-digit numbers from the table with one such number for each period that the classroom economy may be in operation. Then the random number can be converted to an adjustment in the potential sales figure as follows:

If the random number is	Then change the computed potential sales figure by
9	+2
7 or 8	+1
3, 4, 5, or 6	0
1 or 2	−1
0	−2

In other words, consumer demand should first be computed as indicated above. Suppose potential sales would be 88 without any further adjustments. If the random number for that period were 2, then the potential sales figure would be adjusted downward by 1 to 87 and a figure of 87 be announced as potential sales. Any other randomizing device may be used, such as flipping coins or rolling dice, and then associating each possible outcome with some adjustment of potential sales. The suggested adjustments are relatively small and are not likely to make the inference problem in Chapter 6 at all difficult. The teacher may wish to make larger adjustments both to obscure the function he is using and to create greater uncertainty about the direction of the classroom economy at any time.

The one detail left hanging at the end of the previous section is what to announce for potential sales in month 1. If a type-I or type-III function is used, the computational procedures suggested here may be used directly. If a type-II function is used, there is no information about spendable income prior to month 1. In that case, the teacher should arbitrarily select a value for spendable income in the previous period that is somewhere in the vicinity of spendable income in month 1. If he thinks income is likely to drop for the first few months, he might pick a value slightly above spendable income in month 1. If he thinks income will start rising, he could select a slightly lower value. The value chosen does not matter a great deal, since the class, in checking hypothesis II, will neglect the first observation on consumption anyway.

10   PREPARING CLASSROOM INCOME ACCOUNTS

In Chapter 4, the national income figures were obtained by manipulating and summing individual firms' income statements. The classroom economy has been structured in such a way that the figures can be obtained directly from the basic production decisions, orders of materials, and sales of consumer goods. Let:

Q_t = quantity of consumer goods produced
M_t = materials ordered by producers of consumer goods
C_t = total purchases of consumer goods
Y_t = net national product
I_t = net investment in inventories
W_t = wages
R_t = interest and profits (returns to investment goods)

The values of the first three variables (Q_t, M_t, C_t) are found in the totals at the bottom of the classroom economy record. The figure 'for C_t is the level of consumption that goes into the classroom income accounts. The rest of the items in the accounts can be found by means of the following formulas:

$$Y_t = .4\,Q_t + .4\,M_t + .2\,C_t \qquad (5.A.2)$$
$$I_t = .4\,Q_t + .4\,M_t - .8\,C_t \qquad (5.A.3)$$
$$W_t = .4\,Q_t + .2\,M_t + 80.0 \qquad (5.A.4)$$
$$R_t = .2\,M_t + .2\,C_t - 80.0 \qquad (5.A.5)$$

Technology and costs were designed to simplify as much as possible the period-by-period computations of the classroom income accounts. The general procedure for deriving the accounts from income statements of individual firms is presented in Chapter 4. Formulas (5.A.2) to (5.A.5) provide a short-cut path to the same results. To help the reader understand these formulas, we shall present an intuitive explanation rather than a complete derivation.

Y_t denotes total net-value-added in period t. Its value depends on three kinds of decisions. First, every unit of materials ordered sells for $100. Of this, $50 is added to wages and $50 to profits. No additional intermediate products are required when additional units of materials are ordered and produced. Second, every unit of consumer goods produced adds another $100 to value added in the form of wage payments. Third, every unit of consumer goods sold adds $50 to net value added in the form of additions to profit. Since each unit of real net national product is worth $250, it follows that $100 is equivalent to .4 units of real product and $50 is equivalent to .2 units. Thus, Y_t depends on the magnitude of orders for materials M_t, production of consumer goods Q_t, and sales of consumer goods C_t in the proportions indicated by formula (5.A.2).

Formula (5.A.3) can be built up directly by beginning with the definition of net investment in terms of changes in inventories, or indirectly by noting that consumption plus net investment equals net national product. Using the latter approach, we note that the formula for I_t can be obtained by subtracting C_t from the formula for Y_t.

The constant term of 80.0 is in the equation for W_t because the producers of equipment and materials pay a total of $20,000 in wages each period no matter what decisions are made by producers of consumer goods. $20,000 is equivalent to 80 units of real NNP. It was noted above that each unit of consumer goods produced adds $100 to wages while each unit of materials adds $50 to wages. These figures account for the .4 Q_t and .2 M_t, respectively, in formula (5.A.4). Finally, the .2 M_t and .2 C_t in formula (5.A.5) arise from the fact that each unit of materials sold adds $50 to profits as does each unit of consumer goods sold. The -80.0 covers the fixed wage commitments by firms. As a check, note that the sum of the expressions on the right side of the formulas for W_t and R_t gives the formula for Y_t.

As a further check, the teacher should refer back to Table 4.7 in Chapter 4. In that example, 850 units of materials were ordered, 850 units of consumer goods were produced, and 760 units of consumer goods were sold. Formulas (5.A.2) through (5.A.5) should give the same numbers as those shown in Table 4.7. The figures at the bottom of the illustrative Classroom Economy Record were also obtained using these formulas.

Students should be cautioned about care in their own records. An error in carrying over inventories may lead to inappropriate and costly decisions. Managers should try to amass greater profits than the competitors. Finally, the limitations on decisions should be stressed. Production may not exceed materials available.[5] Units sold may not exceed goods available. Materials ordered may not change by more than 20 units from one month to the next. Other than those restrictions anything goes if the managers are convinced that it will help the cumulative profits of their firm vis-à-vis other firms.

After a few periods, the students will begin to get some idea of what is happening in the classroom economy. At that time, the teacher should consider asking for one more bit of information. In Chapter 7 there is a discussion of planned investment, which is important in determining what will be called the temporary equilibrium of the economy. Planned investment can be readily determined if the managers record their forecasts of potential sales. In other words, it will be useful later if the managers of each firm hand in an estimate of what they think potential sales will be during the period along with their production and ordering decisions.

---

[5]In the text, capacity has been considered to be 100 units of output. Some upper limit is needed, but for an actual run of the classroom economy it may be desirable to allow production to run higher in order to avoid having an expansion choked off too soon by a low ceiling on productive capacity. An announcement of any limit to the class is sufficient. Nothing in the bookkeeping needs to be changed.

6

ANALYSIS OF CONSUMER BEHAVIOR

Each class will observe behavior in a particular classroom economy. In a large class, data will be available for several economies. One economy may experience a severe depression, another a boom. Some may remain in stationary states, and others may have cycles of business activity. Economic theory should be able to provide a plausible explanation for whatever the observations may have been.

The operation of an economy involves interaction. Appropriate decisions and actions depend on the present situation, what others are doing and expectations about the future. Thus, the immediate outcome for any decision-maker is the result not only of his own actions but also of events beyond his direct control. To whatever extent is feasible, he would like to be able to predict these external events.

Consider the classroom economy. Managers of firms producing consumer goods make decisions at the beginning of a period. The outcome, in this case potential sales, depends on consumer decisions, which managers would like very much to forecast accurately. Rule of thumb forecasts may work, but it is desirable to understand why they work and under what circumstances they may not work. Toward this end, economists propose hypotheses about determinants of consumer spending and seek evidence for or against each hypothesis. Since the classroom economy does not contain live human beings actively pursuing objectives as members of the household sector, the teacher uses a formula to represent consumer decisions.

The three formulas proposed at the end of Chapter 5 are variations of the plausible hypothesis that disposable income is the primary determinant of consumption expenditures.[1] In Section 6 of this chapter, the students will turn to data from the U.S. economy in an attempt to verify for themselves the relevance of the assumptions made about the consumption function in the theory of income determination. While consumption as a function of income is widely accepted as a valid hypothesis, there are other factors that may be important. Consequently, the emphasis in this chapter is on the problem of selecting among alternative hypotheses.

For the classroom economy, the three hypotheses about the consumption function are:

$$\text{I} \quad C_t^* = A_\text{I} + b_\text{I} Z_t$$

$$\text{II} \quad C_t^* = A_\text{II} + b_\text{II} Z_{t-1}$$

$$\text{III} \quad C_t^* = (A_\text{III} + Dt) + b_\text{III} Z_t$$

The student's problem is to infer from the data which of these functions best describes consumer behavior in his own classroom economy. In other words, what consumption function did the teacher pick?

There are essentially two problems. One is to figure out which *type* of function has been used, and the other is to estimate the parameters in the function. The latter problem will be considered first on the assumption that the type of function is known and that the observations fit at least one of the functions perfectly. The problem of choosing among types of functions will be dealt with subsequently.

1   FITTING A FUNCTION TO DATA

This section shows how to go about finding the parameters of a consumption function if the form of the function is known. In the ensuing discussion, the term *observation* refers to all the relevant data from a single period. Thus, in the classroom economy, a single observation can include both the level of spendable income and the level of consumer demand. The pair of values (Z_1, C_1^*) is an observation of spendable income and consumer demand for month 1. The values (Z_2, C_2^*) constitute an observation for month 2.

If the consumption function is of type I, then two observations with different values are sufficient to determine the values of the parameters

---

[1] If money, or credit, had been introduced explicitly into the classroom economy, it influence on consumer spending could also have been postulated and the set of hypotheses increased accordingly. The same would be true if the structure were even more complicated for example, with prices, wages, technology, or the interest rate subject to change.

A_I and b_I. This will be shown both algebraically and with a numerical example. Suppose $Z_1 = 900$, $C_1^* = 900$, $Z_2 = 920$, and $C_2^* = 916$. This example indicates that when spendable income equals 900, consumer demand also equals 900; and when spendable income is 920, consumer demand is 916.

One way to compute the parameters of type-I function is first to find b_I, the slope of the line. The slope is the change in consumer demand between any two points over the change in spendable income:

$$b_I = \frac{C_2^* - C_1^*}{Z_2 - Z_1} = \frac{\Delta C^*}{\Delta Z} \tag{6.1}$$

In terms of the example, $\Delta C^* = 16$ and $\Delta Z = 20$. The ratio is 16/20, so that $b_I = 8$ is the value of the MPC.

A type-I function can be rewritten in the form:

$$A_I = C_t^* - b_I Z_t \tag{6.2}$$

It is then possible to solve for A_I by substituting the value found for b_I and the values of Z_t and C_t^* from either one of the observations. Using the first observation in the example:

$$A_I = 900 - .8\,(900) = 900 - 720 = 180.$$

Thus, the line that fits the two observations is:

$$C_t^* = 180 + .8\,Z_t.$$

The students can readily check that the second observation does fit this function.

If the consumption function is of type II, then three observations are needed. Consumer demand in period t depends on spendable income in period $t - 1$. With only one observation of consumer demand and spendable income, there is no information about this type of consumption function. With a second observation, there is one point on the function: (Z_1, C_2^*). A third observation is necessary to get a second point on the function: (Z_2, C_3^*). These two points can then be used to find the values of the parameters A_{II} and b_{II}.

Suppose a third observation is added to the two used in the preceding example. The illustrative values are:

t	Z_t	C_t^*
1	900	900
2	920	916
3	932	928

By graphing the points or by repeating the procedure for computing the parameters A_I and b_I but with the second and third observations, the students can verify that a single type-I function does not pass through these three points. For one thing, the MPC between months 2 and 3 is 1.0 instead of the value .8 found between the first two observations.

If these observations were the result of a type-II function, then the values of A_{II} and b_{II} can be calculated in the same manner as that described for the parameters of a type-I function. Consumer demand is 916 when the prior month's spendable income is 900 and it is 928 when prior income is 920. When spendable income goes up by 20 from month 1 to month 2, consumer demand goes up by 12 from month 2 to month 3. This implies an MPC of 12/20, that is, $b_{II} = .6$. The parameter A_{II} can be found by substitution in:

$$A_{II} = C_t^* - b_{II}Z_{t-1}.$$

Thus, using C_2^* and Z_1, we find:

$$A_{II} = 916 - .6\,(900) = 916 - 540 = 376.$$

The type-II function that fits the illustrative data is therefore:

$$C_t^* = 376 + .6\,Z_{t-1}$$

The students should check that C_3^* and Z_2 satisfy this equation.

If the consumption function is of type III, three observations can be used to compute the parameters if there have been different changes in income. The preceding example can also be used to compute A_{III}, D, and b_{III} assuming the data were the result of a type-III consumption function:

$$C_t^* = A_{III} + Dt + b_{III}Z_t$$

For the previous period, the function can be written:

$$C_{t-1}^* = A_{III} + D(t-1) + b_{III}Z_{t-1}$$

Substracting the second expression from the first:

$$C_t^* - C_{t-1}^* = D + b_{III}(Z_t - Z_{t-1}),$$

which can be written more compactly as:

$$\Delta C^* = D + b_{III}\Delta Z$$

To show how this expression can be used to find the values of b_{III} and D, consider the example. Consumer demand increases by 16 when spendable income goes up by 20, and it rises by 12 when income rises by 12. These values can be substituted for ΔC^* and ΔZ to obtain the following two equations:

$$16 = D + 20\,b_{III}$$

$$12 = D + 12\,b_{III}$$

Subtract the second equation from the first:

$$4 = 8\, b_{\text{III}}$$

Solve for b_{III} and substitute back to find D. The solution values are $b_{\text{III}} = .5$ and $D = 6$. It is then posisble to find A_{III} by substitution in the equation:

$$A_{\text{III}} = C_t^* - Dt - b_{\text{III}}Z_t$$

Using the observation when $t = 1$,

$$A_{\text{III}} = 900 - 6 - .5\,(900) = 894 - 450 = 444.$$

Thus, the type-III function that fits the illustrative data is:

$$C_4^* = 444 + 6t + .5\, Z_t$$

Students should check that this also fits the observations when $t = 2$ and $t = 3$.

The fact that the same set of three observations could have come from either a type-II or a type-III consumption function suggests that four different observations will generally be necessary to decide which of the three functions is consistent with the data. The way to distinguish between the type-II and type-III functions is to see which one a fourth observation fits. For example, $C_4^* = 935.2$ is consistent witht he type-II function. Why? If $Z_4 = 942$ and $C_4^* = 939$, then the type-III function is the one being used. All of this assumes that every observation will satisfy one and only one of the three functions after a sufficient number of observations become available.

2 RANDOM DEVIATIONS

If none of the functions fits perfectly, what should be done? There are three possibilities: (1) somebody made a mistake; (2) the teacher is trying some other function; (3) observations do not always lie exactly on the function. If there has been a mistake, it can be corrected. If the instructor is trying another function, he may want to let the students stew for awhile to see if they can explain consumer behavior for themselves.

Even when there has been no mistake and no other type of function is being used, the method of computing potential sales almost guarantees that observations will not be exactly on the consumption function. This is due to the procedure of rounding individual potential sales to the nearest integer. There is the possibility of still another complication. The teacher may have added a random term to the consumption function. For example, under hypothesis I the consumption function can be written as follows:

$$C_t^* = A_{\text{I}} + b_{\text{I}}Z_t + u_t \qquad (6.6)$$

where u_t is a random variable.

A variable, unlike a constant, can take on any of a number of possible values. Spendable income Z_t is an example of a variable. A random variable is a variable for which there is a probability attached to each of its possible values. As a simple example, suppose the random variable u_t may have any one of the three values -10, 0, or $+10$ in period t. Suppose also that a coin is tossed twice to determine which of these values may occur. If it shows tails both times, $u_t = -10$; if there is one heads and one tails, $u_t = 0$; and if both are heads, $u_t = +10$. The possible outcomes of the coin tossing and the associated values of u_t are:

First Toss	*Second Toss*	*Value of u_t*
Tails	Tails	-10
Tails	Heads	0
Heads	Tails	0
Heads	Heads	$+10$

If each of these four outcomes of tossing the coin is equally likely, the probability of each is 1/4. For every value of u_t there is associated a probability:

Value of u_t	*Probability of Occurring*
-10	$\frac{1}{4}$
0	$\frac{1}{2}$
$+10$	$\frac{1}{4}$

This example can now be interpreted in terms of the consumption function (6.6). Imagine a coin tossing experiment to determine the value of u_t in each period. Over a number of periods, about one-fourth of the time potential sales will be lower by 10 (one per firm) than it would be in terms of $A_1 + b_1 Z_t$, and about one-fourth of the time consumer demand will be 10 higher than if it were determined by the same function without the random variable.

The Appendix to Chapter 5 contains a table in which (with ten firms) the value of u_t can be -20, -10, 0, 10, or 20 depending on what numbers are found when the teacher consults a table of random numbers. In this case there is 1 chance in 10 (for a probability of 1/10) that u_t will be -20, 2 chances in 10 (for a probability of 1/5) that u_t will be -10, and so on. The teacher does not know which value u_t will take on in any period until after he has consulted the table of random numbers.

This does not mean that consumers necessarily flip coins, roll dice, or consult a table of random numbers before they make their spending decisions. The reason for this approach rests in a belief that there are factors other than total income that influence total consumption. Personal wealth, the household sector's stock of durable goods, political events, distribution of income, credit conditions, and households' expectations about the future are just a few examples of possible influences on the level of consumption at any time. No one denies that these factors can influence consumption.

Economists hypothesize, however, that changes in these other factors will cause relatively minor changes in the level of consumption compared with changes caused by variations in levels of income. Furthermore, these other factors are assumed to cause consumption to deviate from the consumption function in a random fashion. There may be a small probability that consumption will be very much above or very much below the "true" consumption function and a larger probability that it will deviate by smaller amounts. The random variable allows one to recognize the fact that not all observations of consumption and income fit perfectly to any simple function, but every little change in consumption does not have to be explained.

When there are these random deviations from the assumed underlying relationship between consumption and income, the problem of inferring which function best describes consumer behavior becomes more difficult than when each observation fits the actual function perfectly. There are statistical techniques for testing hypotheses, but they are beyond the scope of this book. We shall rely here on the use of graphs.

Table 6.1 Graphical Patterns for the Three Types of Consumption Functions

	Graph of C_t^* and Z_t	Graph of C_t^* and Z_{t-1}
If function is of type I	Points all lie close to a straight line	Points follow a clockwise pattern being higher when income rises than when income falls
If function is of type II	Points follow a counterclockwise pattern, being higher when income falls than when income rises	Points all lie close to a straight line
If function is of type III	Points follow a sharp sawtooth pattern as income rises and falls	Points follow an upward clockwise spiral

86   *Analysis of Consumer Behavior*

3   GRAPHICAL INFERENCES

The procedure in this section will be to consider how data on consumer spending can be used to discern the consumption function. Observations will be plotted on two graphs. One will show consumer demand as a function of spendable income in the same period; the other will show consumer demand as a function of spendable income one period earlier. The comparative results, depending on which consumption function is used, are summarized in Table 6.1. Each of the three hypotheses has its own unique graphical pattern. One can then graph an actual set of observations, look at the pattern, and infer which of the three hypotheses to accept.

Table 6.2 presents four sets of data on consumer demand and spendable income. For each of the first three sets the function is given. The last set, "the mystery guest," must be identified by the class. The values for Z_t in these examples have been chosen arbitrarily to give pictures that include both falling and rising levels of income.

Table 6.2   Examples of Data on Consumer Demand (C_t^*) and Spendable Income (Z_t)

1. $C_t^* = 180 + .8Z_t$

t	Z_t	C_t^*
1	940	930
2	912	910
3	877	880
4	835	850
5	790	810
6	804	820
7	849	860
8	896	900
9	944	940
10	921	920

2. $C_t^* = 273 + .7Z_{t-1}$

t	Z_t	C_t
1	861	880
2	876	880
3	848	890
4	800	870
5	810	830
6	865	840
7	915	880
8	935	910
9	924	930
10	895	920

3. $C_t^* = 328 + 4t + .6Z_t$

t	Z_t	C_t^*
1	800	810
2	818	830
3	847	850
4	884	870
5	935	910
6	920	900
7	898	890
8	874	880
9	861	880
10	893	900

4. *The Mystery Guest*

t	Z_t	C_t^*
1	900	870
2	860	840
3	810	820
4	750	750
5	700	740
6	710	760
7	760	770
8	830	800
9	850	840
10	800	810

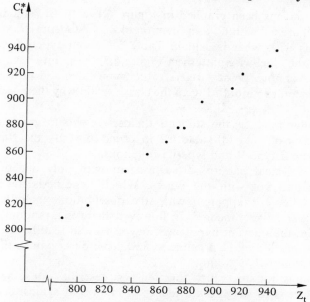

Figure 6.1 Consumer Demand (C_t^*) Plotted as a Function of Z_t Using Data from Part 1 of Table 6.2

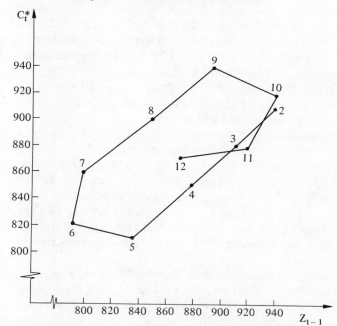

Figure 6.2 C_t^* Plotted as a Function of Z_{t-1} Using Data from Part 1 of Table 6.2

The first set has been graphed in Figure 6.1 with C_t^* as a function of Z_t and in Figure 6.2 with C_t^* as a function of Z_{t-1}. Students should compare these graphs with what is said in Table 6.1 about type-I functions. To help detect the clockwise pattern in Figure 6.2, the points have been numbered. For example, point 2 refers to consumer demand in month 2 and spendable income in month 1. Can the class explain why there is a clockwise pattern?

In a similar manner, the students themselves should graph the second and third sets of data in Table 6.2 in order to verify the statements in Table 6.1 about type-II and type-III functions.

Certain graphical patterns are consistent with only one of the three hypotheses and not with the others. Which hypothesis has been used becomes particularly apparent when the observations include periods of both falling and rising income. If, however, there is a random variable in the function, the relevant hypothesis may not be so readily discerned. For each hypothesis it may be possible to find some observations that are consistent and others that are not.

When one is not sure which function best describes consumer behavior, the procedure is to weigh the evidence in favor and against each, make a tentative selection, and then perhaps wait until there are more observations that tend either to support the conclusion or else to weigh in favor of a different choice. The mystery guest in Table 6.2 is an example in which none of the three hypotheses fits the data perfectly. The data have been graphed in Figures 6.3 and 6.4. It is evident that in neither case do the observations lie on a straight line. With careful inspection of these graphs, however, the observer should conclude that the data are more in accord with a type-I than with either a type-II or type-III function.

The next problem is to estimate the values of the parameters; for without such estimates one cannot say anything about the sensitivity of consumer spending to changes in income nor about the level of the long-run equilibrium. To appreciate the uncertainty engendered by a random term in the consumption function, each student should make his own estimate of A_I and b_I. He should plot the points from part 4 of Table 6.2 on graph paper, as they are in Figure 6.3, draw a straight line that he thinks fits the observations best, mark any two points on this line (as far apart as possible), find the values of income and consumption from the axes of the graph, and use formulas (6.1) and (6.2) to compute the estimates of A_I and b_I.

This done, it is likely that every member of the class has a slightly different set of estimates for the parameters A_I and b_I. Any one of them or none of them may be the actual values that, together with a random variable, were used to generate these observations. This illustrates an important point. *On the basis of data alone one may never be able to estimate the marginal*

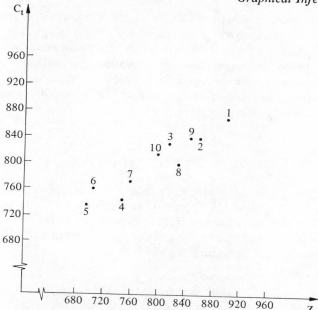

Figure 6.3 C_t^* Plotted as a Function of Z_t Using Data for the Mystery Guest in Table 6.2

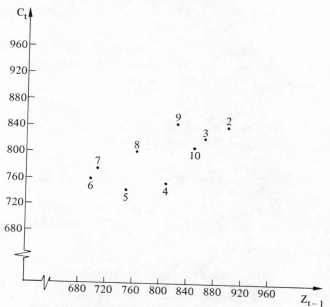

Figure 6.4 C_t^* Plotted as a Function of Z_{t-1} Using Data for the Mystery Guest

propensity to consume with precision, even when it is known that consumption is basically a linear function of income.[2] As a rule, however, the more observations available, the more precisely can the parameters be estimated. Uncertainty exists in almost any attempt to estimate assumed behavioral relationships. Economists try to reduce the extent of their uncertainty as much as possible, but they can rarely be sure. These comments will take on added significance in the discussion in Chapter 8 of appropriate government policies.

4 WHAT CONSUMPTION FUNCTION DID THE TEACHER USE?

The foregoing discussion indicates how estimates of the consumption function may be obtained. This can be an important piece of information in developing an understanding of what happens in a classroom economy. Of even greater importance to the student is an appreciation of the general approach, which can be summarized in four steps:

1. Set forth alternative hypotheses.
2. Derive predicted results that follow *if* each hypothesis is true.
3. Examine the actual observations for evidence that tends to support one hypothesis over the others, that is, evidence that is most likely to have occurred if one of the hypotheses is true.
4. Try to make quantitative estimates of the hypothesized relationship (allowing for some margin of error).

Thus, as new data become available and new hypotheses are suggested the process of testing and, if possible, sharpening estimates continues. In this manner economists try to develop an understanding of various aspects of an economy.

By plotting the available data from their own classroom economy and referring to material in this chapter, the students should try to agree on the consumption function that the teacher has used.

5 CONSUMER BEHAVIOR IN THE U.S. ECONOMY

The foregoing exercise is a prelude to another exercise. The theory of income determination has as one of its assumptions that consumption is a

---

[2]When the consumption function has been judged to be of type III, the coefficients A_{III}, D, and b_{III} are even more difficult to estimate precisely. In fact, with a limited number of periods and a small value for D, it is difficult to distinguish a type-III from a type-I function by graphical inspection. If the instructor or some students in the class are familiar with a multiple regression program, it is well worth spending time having a type-III function fitted to the data, discussing the nature of the estimated coefficients and standard errors, and considering whether to accept or reject the hypothesis that a type-III function is being used.

function of disposable income with the MPC between zero and unity. Do data from the U.S. economy tend to support such an assumption?

A number of points should be noted before the students try to find an answer to this question. Quarterly data on disposable income and consumption can be found in issues of the *Survey of Current Business* (see the reference in Chapter 4). These figures are available in both current dollars and in real (constant dollar) terms. The question of which to use, and why, could open up a whole new set of hypotheses about consumer behavior. Rather than tackle this topic here, assume that the consumption function is in real terms. The data to use are then the constant dollar figures, seasonally adjusted, at annual rates. "Seasonally adjusted, at annual rates" is a way of expressing the quarterly data to reflect what the annual figures would be if the level of activity during a quarter were to continue at the same relative level throughout the other three quarters of the year.

In the classroom economy, consumption figures reported in the accounts can differ from the level of consumer demand whenever some firms have an inadequate supply of goods. There may be a parallel situation at times in the U.S. economy, but there is no announcement about potential sales. In using the reported figures for consumption expenditures, economists must assume that these figures reflect what consumers were planning to buy during that quarter and that events did not frustrate consumer plans to any significant degree.

Each student should pick a period of about five years, so that he will have perhaps 20 observations. Different members of the class may wish to use different periods. The observations on consumption and disposable income should be plotted on graph paper and the graphs used to help answer the following questions:

1. Does consumer spending tend to vary with disposable income?
2. What is the value of the marginal propensity to consume?[3] Is it positive and less than one?
3. Are there any indications that one of the three hypotheses about consumer spending is most in accord with the U.S. data or is none clearly better than the others?
4. Is there any indication that factors other than disposable income have

---

[3]There is a technical problem here that does not arise with data in the classroom economy. If the level of consumption influences the level of income during the same period (as well as the other way around) so that the economy tends each quarter to move from one state of equilibrium to another, then a plot of consumption and income may show a steeper slope than that of the "true" consumption function. This proposition is demonstrated in more advanced courses on statistical estimation of economic relationships. For purposes here it is sufficient to check that consumption and income do tend to move together fairly systematically and not be concerned with more sophisticated manipulation of the data.

exerted a substantial and systematic influence on consumer spending? If so, suggest what those factors might be.

The theory of income determination depends on the assumption that consumption tends to vary directly with changes in income. The foregoing exercise should help the class decide whether or not to accept this assumption. The student who is unwilling to do so should be challenged to find a preferable explanation for consumer spending. We shall proceed as if the assumption is acceptable.

7

DISEQUILIBRIUM, INVESTMENT, AND GROWTH

The next step in developing the theory of income determination is to introduce investment plans by business and the possibility not only that an economy may be out of equilibrium but also that forces may act to change the equilibrium level itself. This chapter analyzes some consequences of changing investment decisions within the business sector. The students' first-hand knowledge of the operation of a classroom economy will be utilized in developing key concepts, but the relevance of the concepts to an understanding of a real economy is of primary concern. The chapter ends with a presentation of data from the U.S. economy over the last four decades.

1 DESIRED STOCK AND PLANNED INVESTMENT

A useful construct in economic analysis is the *desired capital stock*. This is the stock of investment goods that managers would like their firms to have on the basis of their own perception of the present and future state of the market. In a real economy, a great many factors may influence the desired capital stock. The costs of acquiring buildings, equipment, and materials and how these costs are likely to change can make a difference. The present level of demand for various products that a business sells as well as projections of future demand must be taken into account. Impending domestic or international political events may also weigh in an executive's mind as he ponders what kinds of assets his firm needs and should acquire. The state of the labor market and the financial markets can be important too.

As with the consumption function, the classroom economy affords a setting in which the concept of the desired capital stock can be formulated in an elementary manner. Managers in the classroom economy have so far not been given the option of changing their firm's stock of equipment, nor need they worry about changing prices, wages, and borrowing costs. The investment decision has been reduced to decisions about inventory holdings of materials and finished goods; and potential sales has been the only variable that needs to be taken into account in formulating these decisions. Ideally a manager in the classroom economy would like to produce, with no unused materials, as many units of consumer goods as consumers plan to buy from his firm and to have no finished goods carried over in inventory. This requires perfect foresight. Given the fact of uncertainty, the manager may plan a buffer stock of inventories, that is, plan to keep a few more units in inventory than are absolutely necessary, just in case potential sales rise unexpectedly.

Managers of a firm in the classroom economy thus formulate their desired stock of inventories for the beginning of the following period on the basis of anticipated potential sales plus the buffer stock they think it prudent to hold. There may be occasions when inadequate inventories of materials may mean that a firm cannot possibly achieve the desired stock of inventories. In such cases, the managers plan to add as much to inventory as they think is possible. Otherwise, they will plan to add the difference between the desired stock of inventories and the present level. Such decisions define *planned investment* in inventories.

At this point the students should go back and review their decisions as managers. For each period, they should reconstruct, as best they can, how many units they planned to change their stock of materials and holdings of finished goods. (Some teachers may have asked that these plans be recorded while the economy is in operation or that the necessary sales forecasts be made.) For example, if a firm has 75 units of materials at the beginning of a period and orders 85 units, the managers are planning a 10-unit increase in materials. If managers have 5 units of finished goods in inventory at the beginning of the period and plan to produce about 5 units more than they expect to sell, they are planning a 5-unit increase in finished goods inventory. The investment plans for the firm during that period are to add 10 units of materials and 5 units of finished goods.

Each unit of materials is worth .4 units of final consumer goods and each unit of finished goods is worth .8 units of final consumer goods. To convert the investment plans into a single figure that is measured in the same units as NNP, the students should multiply the planned investment in materials by .4 and add to that figure the planned investment in finished goods multiplied by .8. In the example, planned investment becomes .4 (10) + .8 (5) = 8. In other words, the firm in that period plans to add 8 units to its stock of inventories. If every firm can reconstruct what its investment plans were in each period, a series of figures for planned investment can be constructed for the classroom economy as a whole. These data will be useful in subsequent analysis.

One point is important to note. Actual investment may not be the same as planned investment. In trying to reconstruct past investment plans, students may use the actual change in materials. The actual change in finished goods, however, will not be what was planned unless the managers correctly anticipated their firms' sales for the period. If sales are less than expected, finished-goods inventory will be higher than planned. If sales are higher than expected, inventories will be lower than planned. It is the planned change that is to be recorded.

2 TEMPORARY EQUILIBRIUM

Equilibrium occurs when aggregate demand equals aggregate supply. This is the nature of the equilibrium condition (5.2) in Chapter 5. In the absence of any planned investment by business and of changing levels of government demand, this condition can be used to find the economy's position of long-run equilibrium, that is, the stationary state. It is of little help, however, in analyzing short-run adjustments when the economy is in *disequilibrium* (aggregate supply not equal to aggregate demand). Short-run adjustments are further complicated by changes in investment plans by business. The equilibrium condition needs to be expanded beyond the $Y = C$ formulation presented in Chapter 5. Let

I_t = planned investment in period t

If C_t equals consumer demand (ignoring the possibility that some consumer plans may be frustrated), aggregate demand in period t becomes $C_t + I_t$. Inclusion of government demand will be postponed until the next chapter. For now, the equilibrium condition that aggregate supply be equal to aggregate demand can be written:

$$Y_t = C_t + I_t \tag{7.1}$$

Assume that consumption is the following function of net national product:

$$C_t = 230 + .75\, Y_t \tag{7.2}$$

This has been graphed in Figure 7.1 and labeled C. The long-run equilibrium position evidently occurs when Y equals 920. If planned investment is 10, then $C + I$ can be plotted in Figure 7.1 by drawing a line parallel to and 10 units above the consumption function. $C + I$ expressed as a function of Y is now the aggregate demand schedule.

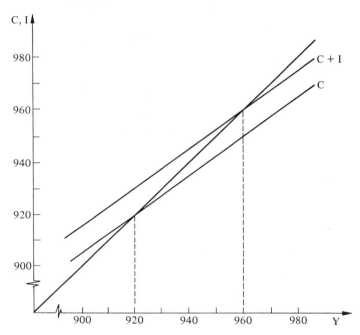

Figure 7.1   An Illustration of the Investment Multiplier and the Determination of a Temporary Equilibrium

If the economy is originally at its long-run equilibrium level of 920 and there is a planned increase of business inventories of 10, net national product might rise to 930, but this would be inadequate to achieve an addition to inventories of 10. The increased income increases consumer demand by 7.5. Only if production is increased all the way to 960 will businesses be successful in their plans to build up inventories by 10.

This is another example of the multiplier. Since consumers, in this example, spend three-fourths of every additional dollar of income, production must be increased by 40 in order to obtain an increase of 10 in investment. The new equilibrium level of income increases by 4 times the upward shift in the aggregate demand schedule. If the marginal propensity to consume had been four-fifths, the multiplier would have been 5. Equilibrium income would have been increased by 50 in response to an increase of 10 in the flow demand by business for an addition to inventories.

No hypothesis has as yet been advanced to explain the determination of investment plans. It has simply been assumed that, at the beginning of period t, firms have made their investment plans. These plans cannot be changed until the beginning of the next period. Planned investment can therefore be treated as a given parameter for the duration of period t.

Suppose the consumption function is the same linear function hypothesized in Chapter 5:

$$C_t = A_t + bY_t \tag{7.3}$$

The only difference is that subscripts have been added to denote the period in which income is received and in which consumption takes place. The subscript on the A parameter indicates that the consumption function itself may shift from one period to another.

The equations (7.1) and (7.3) are two equations in the two unknowns C_t and Y_t. These can be readily solved for Y_t. Figure 7.1 illustrates the graphical solution. The algebraic procedure is to substitute in equation (7.1) for C_t from equation (7.3) and solve explicitly for Y_t:

$$\bar{Y}_t = \frac{A_t + I_t}{1 - b} \tag{7.4}$$

As before, the bar over the Y_t term indicates that this is the value that satisfies an equilibrium condition, given the assumed consumption function and the level of planned investment. We call this a *temporary equilibrium* level of net national product. It is temporary because its value will change from period to period as the level of planned investment changes.

In the example with the consumption function (7.2), $A = 230$, $b = .75$, $I_t = 10$. It follows from formula (7.4) that $\bar{Y}_t = 960$. With actual net national product below this level, there is an excess demand and inventories will be increased by less than the desired 10 units. Production must be increased by still more (toward the temporary equilibrium) if inventories are to be increased at the rate of 10 per period. Above equilibrium, the firms will be adding more than 10 units per period and will tend to cut orders and production, thus moving the economy back toward its equilibrium level. Only at $Y = 960$ can inventories be increased by 10 every period.

The perceptive reader may have noticed an inconsistency in the foregoing argument. A decision to increase inventories by 10 is undoubtedly motivated by a desire to have the desired *stock* of inventories 10 higher; but once that objective has been achieved, why would firms continue to add to their inventories? Investment is a flow, an addition to the capital stock that is, the stock of investment goods) per unit of time. Even if the temporary equilibrium is never reached, the planned additions to inventories may be accomplished in the course of two or three periods. In the example, NNP of 960 cannot be a stationary state since the desire to add to inventories is inconsistent with a constant level of production period after period.

There is only one level of planned investment that is fully compatible with the stationary state, and that is when planned net investment is zero. Any plans to continue adding to the stock of investment goods make sense only if the economy continues to grow. A plan to continue running down the stock is consistent only with continuing declines in production and sales.

An economy may or may not be in a temporary equilibrium, for equilibrium occurs when aggregate demand and aggregate supply are equal. The nature of the adjustments that will be made when an economy is in disequilibrium depends on the circumstances of supply and demand at the time. Quantity adjustments are considered in the next two sections. The possibility of price adjustments is introduced in Section 5. The concept of a temporary equilibrium is of use primarily in the absence of a more fully developed *dynamic* theory, that is, a theory about how past events influence and determine the present state of affairs and how the present will evolve into the future.

3 INVESTMENT PLANS AND DYNAMIC ADJUSTMENTS

Is it possible to develop a dynamic theory that will explain what happens in a classroom economy? What is needed is the formulation of good hypotheses about managers' behavior. Formulating hypotheses about what determines orders of materials and production decisions represents a real challenge. There is no rigged function here as there was for the consumption function. Each student who has acted as a manager knows something of the factors influencing his own decisions. Perhaps he can suggest hypotheses that would account for the observed changes in aggregate supply over a number of periods. Only when one can say what determines the supply as well as the demand for the final product does the behavior of the classroom economy become explainable.

Knowing what determines the behavior of managers, in addition to the spending decisions by consumers, we can predict future changes that will take place in the economy. To illustrate, suppose that managers of all ten firms in a classroom economy have formulated and will follow the same simple decision rules:

1. Produce just enough to have available for sale 10 units more than last period's potential sales, and
2. Order exactly enough so that materials available next period will be 10 units more than last period's potential sales (within the constraint that an order of materials may not be changed by more than 20 units from one period to the next).

No one advocates these rules nor suggests that firms will use them. What will be illustrated is that if the managers' decisions follow some quantifiable rules, then the course of events becomes predictable.

Table 7.1 has been prepared on the assumption that managers follow these two rules and consumers spend in accordance with equation (7.2) except that Z_t (spendable income) as defined in the appendix to Chapter 5 has been substituted for Y_t. The output and ordering decisions have been imposed arbitrarily in period 1. Each firm begins period 2 with 100 units of materials and 25 units of finished goods in inventory. According to rule 1, each firm will plan to have 102 units of goods available (10 units above potential sales of 92 in period 1). With 25 units in inventory, production of 77 will give the firm its 102 units available for sale. If each firm uses only 77 units of materials, there are 23 units unused. Rule 2 calls for 102 units available for the beginning of period 3 and so each firm orders 79 units of materials. Potential sales in period 2 turn out to be 82 per firm.

The rest of Table 7.1 has been constructed in the same manner until period 7. By period 7, the stupidity of these particular rules becomes apparent. The firms have run out of inventories and are limited in their production by the materials available. As a result, potential sales exceed units available and the firms miss sales.

The foregoing example shows the results of one set of decision rules by producers and consumers. Once the initial conditions are specified and it is known precisely how decision makers are going to react to events, there is no serious difficulty in writing out the sequence of events that will take place. The problem, however, is in developing hypotheses about managers' reactions to events and having those hypotheses appear at all consistent with observations. In the example, the managers were assumed to follow a very rigid set of rules. In any classroom economy, there will always be some managers trying to outguess their competitors. They may anticipate or even try to precipitate a change in the direction of production and sales. Some may keep inventories very close to what is needed. Others may be willing to pay the interest cost of ample inventories. The rules may differ from downswing to upswing. Some managers may be very good at forecasting potential sales; others may be continually making wrong guesses. In other words, even within the simple structure of the classroom economy, a variety of decision rules may be operating at any point in time and very likely changing over time.

Thus, it is virtually impossible to predict with precision what each manager is going to decide each period. Here is where a macroeconomic approach may be useful. With enough decision-makers, one manager's decision to keep production unusually high will tend to be offset by another's decision that it is time to work off excessive inventories quickly. Hypotheses about the average reaction of a group of decision makers to specified situations may provide good approximations to actual totals

Table 7.1

Period No.	(1) Inventory of Materials	(2) Units Produced	(3) Materials Unused (1) − (2)	(4) Materials Ordered	(5) Inv. of Finished Goods	(6) Units Produced	(7) Units Available (5) + (6)	(8) Potential Sales
1	1000	920	80	920	250	920	1170	920
2	1000	770	230	790	250	770	1020	820
3	1020	720	300	620	200	720	920	730
4	920	640	280	550	190	640	830	680
5	830	630	200	580	150	630	780	690
6	780	700	80	710	90	700	790	760
7	790	790	0	860	30	790	820	860

even when an individual's decisions appear highly unpredictable. We shall develop one such macroeconomic hypothesis.

Until there is a fully satisfactory and self-contained theory of the evolution of economic decisions, the concept of a temporary equilibrium can be used to explain why an economy may experience a boom or a depression, or simply remain in a stationary state.

This point can be illustrated by reference to the classroom economy, by using the example underlying Table 7.1. Suppose in this case that managers always maintain the naïve belief that potential sales this month will be the same as potential sales last month. It follows that the decision rule to have available for sale 10 units more than last period's potential sales implies that the desired stock of finished goods inventories for each firm is always 10 units. A firm's planned additions to inventory of finished goods is therefore the difference between 10 and the current level.

At the beginning of period 2, the firms are holding 250 units of finished goods and desire 100. This is a planned disinvestment of 150 units (15 units per firm). They are also planning to increase inventories of materials by 20 from 1000 to 1020. Since each unit of finished goods is worth .8 and each unit of materials is worth .4, the planned investment comes to:

$$(-150)(.8) + (20)(.4) = -120 + 8 = -112$$

In this manner a series of figures for planned investment has been generated. Given planned investment, the temporary equilibrium level can be found by means of formula (7.4). These figures are designated by $\bar{Y}_t$ in Table 7.2. The actual level of net national product in each period is also shown in this table in the column headed $\bar{Y}_t$.

In period 1, net national product is 920. If, in period 2, firms are to be successful in working off 112 worth of inventories, Y has to drop all the

Table 7.2   An Example of Adjustments from Positions of Disequilibrium

t	I_t	$\bar{Y}_t$	Y_t
1			920
2	−112	472	788
3	−120	440	682
4	−108	488	612
5	−60	680	622
6	12	968	716
7	84	1256	824

NOTE: This material is based on data from Table 7.1.

way to 472 before disinvestment can occur at a rate of 112.[1] There is a big drop from period 1 to period 2 but not enough to decrease inventory by 112. At the beginning of period 3 planned investment is -120. The equilibrium level at which investment would continue at a rate of -120 is 440, still well below the actual level of 788 in period 2, and net national product falls to 682 in period 3.

By the beginning of period 5, equilibrium has risen above the actual level; and net national product starts to rise. For the next few periods the temporary equilibrium level is above the actual level. As a result there is a sustained rise in net national product that tends to carry the temporary equilibrium well above the long-run equilibrium level of 920.

This is just one example, and one with fairly simple-minded decision rules, but the results are suggestive. In the classroom economy there are no opportunities to change prices. Consequently, reactions to a position of disequilibrium must be made by quantity adjustments. Notice in Table 7.1 that orders, production, and sales are all equal in period 1. Aggregate demand equals aggregate supply, and the economy is in temporary equilibrium. Managers, however, decide that inventory levels are too high, so they plan to disinvest, that is, they plan to run down the stock of investment goods. This shifts the aggregate demand schedule downward. Because of the multiplier of 4, the equilibrium NNP is lowered by 4 times the downward shift in aggregate demand. Orders and production are cut, moving the economy toward the lower equilibrium level, but the cuts are not sufficient to achieve equilibrium in one period. In this case, the movement is toward, but not to, equilibrium. Decisions in the next month call for new investment plans; the temporary equilibrium changes; and there are adjustments toward the new equilibrium level.

These considerations lead to the following hypothesis about aggregate supply. When aggregate demand exceeds aggregate supply, in which case NNP is below equilibrium, NNP will be adjusted upward. When NNP is above equilibrium, NNP will be adjusted downward. If they are fairly close together, there will be little change in NNP. Since there is a profit incentive for firms to adjust toward the temporary equilibrium level, managers make decisions that guide the economy in that direction.

The rate of adjustment depends on both institutional and psychological factors. In the classroom economy, the rule that orders of materials may not be changed by more than 20 per firm per period is an institutional restriction that may slow the adjustment process. The extent to which managers fail to anticipate the necessary changes or to act accordingly is an example of a psychological factor. Each manager is unwilling to make

---

[1]The figure of 472 is obtained from equation (7.4) with $I = -112$, $A = 230$, $b = .75$. Thus, $\overline{Y} = (230 - 112)/(1 - .75) = 118/.25 = 472$. Similar computations result in the other entries for $\overline{Y}_t$ in Table 7.2.

a rash change knowing full well that all the others are going to make moderate changes too. Any change that is unusually great can mean unnecessary inventories or missed sales. Thus, an economy may not jump directly to its temporary equilibrium.

Imagine a dog trying to catch a rabbit in a large, walled but otherwise open field. If the rabbit sits still the dog can run straight to the rabbit. A desire for self-preservation will likely impel the rabbit to take off in some direction away from the dog. When he comes to a wall, the rabbit will have to veer off in another direction. At this point the dog must maneuver himself around to be once again in pursuit. The path of the dog is evidently influenced by the location of the rabbit. At the same time the course of the rabbit is very much influenced by the actions of the pursuing dog.

Suppose one were asked to explain why the dog (NNP) is heading in a given direction. The answer is simple. He is trying to get to the rabbit (temporary equilibrium). However, the ultimate capture (long-run equilibrium) is largely irrelevant to the present direction of the dog. If at any moment we know the location of both the rabbit and dog, we can say with some certainty which way the dog will go. How much harder it would be to develop a theory that will predict the dog's (and the rabbit's) path for the next ten minutes. This analogy illustrates why economists fall back on the equilibrium concept in the absence of a good theory of dynamic adjustments.

If the teacher has obtained from the students a series of figures for planned investment, as suggested in Section 1, he can present the consumption function he has used (unless the students are still trying to guess the function) and have the students compute the temporary equilibrium level of NNP for each period by means of formula (7.4). They should substitute the values of A_I, A_II, or $A_\text{III} + Dt$ for A_t, and b_I, b_II, or b_III for b depending on whether the function is of type I, II, or III, respectively. The classroom income accounts provide figures for Y_t. It is then possible to see the extent to which this particular classroom economy tended to adjust toward its temporary equilibria.[2]

There are two questions about the stability of the classroom economy. One may be answered by the foregoing considerations. Does the economy tend to adjust toward its temporary equilibrium? The other concerns long-run stability. Is the economy likely eventually to settle into its long-run equilibrium level when a type-I or type-II consumption function has been used or onto its equilibrium path (described in Section 7 below) when a type-III function has been used? If so, how soon? We leave it to the class to speculate on the answers. In the process additional insights

---

[2]For some evidence that adjustments in the U.S. economy may be viewed in this manner, see J. A. Carlson, "Forecasting Errors and Business Cycles," *American Economic Review*, June 1967, pp. 462–481.

may develop as to why certain things happen in a simple economy of th
sort. For example, can the concept of a temporary equilibrium be used
explain why or when a depression will end?

4   THE ACCELERATOR

In the operation of the classroom economy, investment in equipme
has been restricted to replacement of that which wears out. What wou
happen if this restriction did not exist? Would it make any difference in t
adjustment process? An addition to the stock of durable investment goo
is called *fixed investment* to distinguish it from investment in inventori
Allowing managers to choose the level of fixed investment for their fi
will tend to aggravate a depression and stimulate a boom. We show th
first by an example and then consider why.

With the illustrative consumption function presented in Section
the stationary state is at $Y = 920$. In this stationary state each firm is pr
ducing 92 units of output in every period. If the firm has 200 units of equi
ment, there is excess capacity, since it needs only 184 units of equipme
to produce 92 units of output. Whenever firms have excess capacity th
will not be needed in the near future, there is no incentive to replace t
equipment that wears out.

Suppose the managers are given the option to order any amount
new equipment they wish each period, including none at all. With plen
of excess capacity, they will surely order none at all. Assume that $12
worth of equipment per firm wears out each month. Twelve hundr
dollars is worth 4.8 units of real net national product. If all ten firms sudde
ly stop replacing worn-out equipment, there will be a drop of 48 in r
national product. This lowers the wages, interest, and profits paid to t
household sector. If there is a positive MPC, consumption, in turn, w
fall. Table 7.3 contains an example along the same lines as the one
Table 7.1. There is the same consumption function except that spendal
income has been lowered by 48. The same decision rules have been appli
for the orders of materials and the output of consumer goods.

The depression is far more severe than in the previous example. T
difference is that planned investment in equipment in this example is nc
-48. With a multiplier of 4, the temporary equilibrium is lowered by 1
as a result. For as long as producers of consumer goods do not order a
equipment, the temporary equilibrium level of net national product (
the absence of planned inventory investment) will be 728 instead of 92
Inventories are going to continue rising while net national product
above this level. Therefore, unless the economy can reach this tempora
equilibrium level of 728 while capacity is being reduced, there will

Table 7.3

Period No.	Inventory of Materials	Units Produced	Materials Unused (1) − (2)	Materials Ordered	Inv. of Finished Goods	Units Produced	Units Available (5) + (6)	Potential Sales
1	1020	920	100	920	100	920	1020	880
2	1020	840	180	800	140	840	980	810
3	980	740	240	670	170	740	910	720
4	910	630	280	540	190	630	820	630
5	820	540	280	450	190	540	730	570
6	730	510	220	450	160	510	670	570
7	670	530	140	510	120	530	650	550
8	650	610	40	640	70	610	680	660

inventory accumulation. In order to work off these additional inventories, production must go still lower. If this decline were to cause other manufacturers, such as producers of materials and equipment, to stop ordering equipment, the depression could become even worse.

Chapter 9 discusses some possible influences mitigating a real depression, but an important principle is illustrated here. It should be examined carefully. In Figure 7.2, values for net national product from the first example

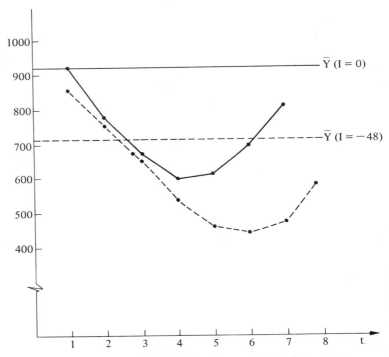

Figure 7.2   An Illustration of How Changes in Fixed Investment
May Influence Cyclical Swings in an Economy

are plotted and connected by solid lines. There is also a solid line for the equilibrium level of Y when planned investment is zero. The dashed line connect the values of net national product in the second example when planned investment in equipment is equal to -48. The equilibrium line for Y when $I = -48$ has also been indicated by a dashed line. In the second case net national product has to fall much farther before firms can work off unwanted inventories.

In both examples, by period 9, inventories have become so small that the firms are going to miss sales in the upswing. This unsatisfied demand will be even greater as soon as the managers begin to order equipment again. Once they decide to increase capacity, the temporary equilibrium will be shifted well above 920 by planned investment in equipment as well as in inventories. A positive planned investment in equipment may further thwart attempts to obtain adequate inventories.

The important point here is that the greater the *capital requirements* per unit change in planned output, the more unstable the economy may be (that is, its fluctuations are likely to be greater) and the long-run equilibrium may be more difficult to attain. By capital requirements is meant the amount of investment that is needed to make possible a change in the level of output. In the classroom economy, if a firm is going to increase production by 5 units it needs 5 more units of materials than it has been using. Five units of materials are equivalent to only 2 unts of real net national product. The investment to make possible the changed production in the next period has only a minor impact on income and sales.

If, however, the firm had to change its capacity by 5 units (that is, by 10 pieces of equipment), this would be an investment on the order of 48 units of real net national product. Small changes in planned output could have sizeable repercussions on demand through the income-generating effect of planned investment. With such high capital requirements, the long-run equilibrium will be exceedingly difficult to attain and may never be reached. The numbers in these examples need not be taken seriously, but the general relationships suggest something about real economies. The economy with the more well-developed industrial process with large amounts of capital per unit of final product has a greater potential instability. One would therefore expect business cycles to be associated more with industrialized than with pre-industrialized economies.

The ratio between the desired increase in the capital stock (that is, the planned level of investment) and the corresponding increase in output is known as the *accelerator*. It represents the amount of investment that will be induced per unit of planned change in output. In the first example the ratio of added capital to an increase in monthly output of consumer goods is .4 to 1. In the second example, it is 10 to 1 (9.6 for equipment plus .4 for materials). If there is some such ratio, whatever its value, then *the greater the rate of growth in output, the higher will be the level of investment*. The analogy can be drawn to the accelerator of an automobile. The faster the speed that a driver wishes to maintain, the farther in he must hold the accelerator pedal. Conversely, investment may experience relatively wide swings if the economy cannot maintain a steady growth. These changes in investment then have a further impact through the multiplier effects that shift the temporary equilibrium levels of NNP. This is sometimes called the interaction between the multiplier and the accelerator.

5   A POSSIBILITY OF INFLATION

A general and continuing increase of prices over a period of time has come to be known as *inflation*. In the discussion of real net national product in Chapter 4, it was noted that prices went up by 17.3 percent between 1958 and 1967. This does not mean that the price of everything rose by 17.3 percent. The prices of some items even went down. The figure of 17.3 percent is based on an average change in the prices of the goods and services that went into net national product in those years. Two other examples of measures of price changes are given in Section 9 below.

Price changes have been ignored in the theory of income determination as presented so far. Part of the reason is that the theory has been based on the assumption that spending decisions are made in real terms. If prices and incomes were all to increase by (say) 10 percent, it is assumed that consumers would not change the quantity and composition of the goods and services consumed, and that business investment plans would not change in real terms. Whether or not these are valid assumptions for the U.S. economy, the question remains: under what circumstances will prices change? The answer, as indicated above, depends on the conditions of supply and demand in markets throughout the economy.

Suppose aggregate demand and aggregate supply are not equal. This means that quantity demanded and quantity supplied are unequal in at least one market, and perhaps in many markets, in the economy. Price theory textbooks go through the cases in which the market adjustments will involve primarily price changes, primarily quantity changes, or changes of both kinds. It would be out of place to go through those here. We have assumed that conditions of supply are such that shifts in demand will result in quantity adjustments, but there is one situation in which quantity adjustments are impossible in the short run. This occurs when demand exceeds what the business sector is able to make available. In that case, it is profitable for suppliers to raise prices and they will likely do so if there is no law against such action. Thus, when quantity demanded in some market exceeds the quantity of goods that suppliers can produce and sell at the going price, given their stock of investment goods and available labor, the price will tend to rise in that market.

If there is excess demand in many markets, we say there are *inflationary pressures*. Prices will rise in response to these pressures. As prices rise there are also pressures to raise wages in labor markets. General and continued excess demand can therefore be an important cause of inflation.[3]

---

[3]It is tacitly assumed that the money supply will be expanded sufficiently to sustain the inflation. A fuller treatment of the subject of inflation would have to consider money explicitly as well as other influences on supply, demand, and market adjustments.

Presumably the reverse process could work when demand falls off, but it may not. If businesses respond to decreased demand by cuts in production and are unable or unwilling to cut wages, then the process is not reversible. Prices will rise in response to sustained excess demand when producers are operating at or close to full capacity and will level off after demand drops. As depicted in Section 9 below, the history of price changes in the U.S. economy over the last forty years provides support for this view.

6 THE CAPITAL-OUTPUT RATIO

This section begins a transition from problems in short-run adjustments to an analysis of the possibility of a steady long-run growth. The first step in this transition will be to change the focus to periods of a year.

If the classroom economy were to use its full capacity to produce consumer goods, the NNP would be 1000 units per month (with ten firms), or 12,000 per year. At $250 per unit this full capacity output would have a dollar value of $3 million. It is easy to verify from the original description of the classroom economy that the total initial value of capital equipment is $6 million. Ignoring inventories, this gives a ratio of capital to annual output of 2 to 1. The ratio is known as the *capital-output ratio*.

The capital-output ratio for the economy as a whole obviously depends on the composition of output if different producers have different capital-output ratios. Define output as net value added. It is then possible to go back to the description of the classroom economy to verify, when the economy is in a stationary state, producing consumer goods at full capacity, that the ratios are:

	Capital-Output Ratio
Consumer goods	1.45
Materials	2.08
Capital goods	6.25
All producers	2.00

If the proportion of these different products changes, the ratio for all producers will also change. The latter ratio can be worked out for any composition of output, but for expository convenience we shall assume a ratio of 2 throughout our discussion of the growth potential of the classroom economy.

For comparative purposes, consider the estimates of some similar ratios for the U.S. economy:[4]

[4]Bert G. Hickman, *Investment and U.S. Economic Growth*, (Washington, D.C.: Brookings Institution, 1965).

Capital-Output Ratio

Total manufacturing	.70
Communications	1.91
Railroads	4.57
All industries covered	1.09

7 INVESTMENT AND GROWTH

Investment has two distinctly different effects. One is its effect on aggregate demand. Production of investment goods results in income. Other things equal, the greater the amount of investment goods produced, the greater will be the income of the household sector; and, with a positive marginal propensity to consume, higher income will induce greater demand for consumer goods. This is the *demand-generating effect* of investment. The higher investment is, the greater the demand for consumer goods, and the higher will be the temporary equilibrium level of net national product.

The other aspect to investment is its *capacity-creating effect*. Discussion of this effect gets to the heart of why producers invest in new capital goods in the first place. They invest in order to increase their output at a later date in the belief that it will be profitable to do so. Thus, the greater the amount of investment activity at the present time, the greater will be the economy's capacity to produce goods and services in the future. For any economy to maintain an orderly growth, just the right amount of new aggregate demand must be assured as the new capacity to produce becomes available.

There are numerous problems in promoting growth, but a necessary condition is that some of the NNP be available for investment. To illustrate the nature of the requisite balance between these two aspects to investment, imagine a classroom economy in which additions to equipment can take place. The analysis will be on an annual basis. Initially the economy has a capacity to produce 12,000 units per year. Let the annual consumption function be:

$$C_t = 1200 + .8\ Y_t,$$

where C_t is annual consumption and Y_t is annual NNP.

The students should check that: (1) the stationary state is at a level of NNP equal to 6000 per year, and (2) with a planned net investment of 1200, the temporary equilibrium becomes 12,000 per year. Note carefully this result. In order to get the aggregate demand schedule up to a point where the equilibrium equals the economy's full-capacity potential to produce, there must be just the right amount of planned investment. Not only that, but the investment increases future capacity. Ever-increasing levels of investment are then needed if equilibrium is to continue to equal the full-capacity level of output.

This can be demonstrated algebraically. Let

$$K_t = \text{the stock of capital equipment available for production in year } t.$$

Assume a capital-output ratio of 2. This means that $K_t/Y_t = 2$, that is,

$$Y_t = K_t/2$$

if capacity is fully utilized. The temporary equilibrium in year t is given by equation (7.4):

$$\bar{Y}_t = \frac{A + I_t}{1 - b}$$

If $\bar{Y}_t$ is to equal full-capacity output, then $\bar{Y}_t$ must equal $K_t/2$, that is,

$$\frac{A + I_t}{1 - b} = \frac{K_t}{2} \tag{7.5}$$

From this expression it is apparent that as K_t grows so too must I_t grow to assure full-capacity equilibrium. Since investment is an addition to the stock of investment goods, or capital equipment, the next year's stock will be:

$$K_{t+1} = K_t + I_t.$$

If I_t is positive, K_{t+1} is greater than K_t. It follows from (7.5) that I_{t+1} must be greater than I_t. With no change in A or b, investment evidently needs to grow larger and larger every year.

In the example, $K_1 = 24,000$, $b = .8$, and $A = 1200$. By equation (7.5):

$$\frac{1200 + I_1}{.2} = 12,000$$

$$1200 + I_1 = 2400$$

$$I_1 = 1200$$

If there is 1200 worth of investment in year 1, the stock of capital equipment grows by 1200 to 25,200 in year 2, and full capacity output grows by 600 to 12,600. For full-capacity equilibrium in year 2, it is necessary that:

$$\frac{1200 + I_2}{.2} = 12,600$$

$$1200 + I_2 = 2520$$

$$I_2 = 1320$$

which is larger than the 1200 needed in year 1.

The example can be carried forward, but the numbers are not important.[5] The main point is that the demand-generating and capacity-creating effects of investment must be properly balanced to assure a steady full-capacity growth. To appreciate this point, try to imagine what would happen if the relationship given in equation (7.5) did not hold. If I_t is too small, equilibrium occurs at less than full capacity:

$$\bar{Y}_t < K_t/2$$

Producers are not so likely to invest as much, that is, add as much to capacity, when existing capacity is unused as when capacity is fully utilized, especially if demand is expected to grow. If investment falls, equilibrium falls, and there may be further cuts in production of the sort discussed in Section 4 in connection with the concept of the accelerator.

Conversely, if investment is too large, so that equilibrium is above full capacity:

$$\bar{Y}_t > K_t/2$$

This is a situation in which aggregate demand is greater than the quantity of goods that the business sector can make available. While price changes have been ruled out in the classroom economy, they have been discussed informally in Section 5. Imagine the reaction of producers if demand exceeds their capacity to produce. Besides raising prices if feasible, they will want greater capacity. This can increase the demand for investment goods and thus aggravate the inflationary pressures.

The conclusion of this section is that investment may be able to grow at just the right rate to sustain a steady growth; but if the balance is upset one way or the other, there are possibilities of a severe depression or serious inflation. This conclusion neglects other possible factors influencing the economy, for example, relative price and wage changes, interest rate changes, and government fiscal policy. We are saying that in an economy with price and wage rigidities (at least downward rigidities), with fairly rigid market shares, with managers not willing to sacrifice their own firms for the good of others, and with consumption as an unchanging function of income, no uninterrupted growth is likely to occur even though long-run growth is theoretically possible.

8 EQUILIBRIUM PATH WITH GROWING DEMAND

Are there any reasons to expect the amount of consumption out of any level of income to shift up with time? We offer the following brief arguments

[5]It may be verified that the algebraic solution to this problem can be written:

$$I_t = \left(1 + \frac{1-b}{2}\right)^{t-1}\left[\frac{(1-b)K_1}{2} - A\right]$$

without providing any empirical support. In the process of economic growth, people save and accumulate wealth. Since wealth imparts a greater sense of economic security, people become willing to spend more at the same level of income. New products stimulate greater consumption. The growing urbanization and complexity of life require higher expenditures. Over time the standard of living rises and many people feel compelled to keep up.

Arguments of the foregoing type can be embellished and developed, but no matter how effectively they may be presented, the student should not thereby be convinced that there is an upward shifting consumption function unless empirical evidence substantiates the claim. All of these arguments represent hypotheses about the way things may be. They suggest the plausibility of the hypotheses and perhaps justify further empirical investigation, but a priori reasoning is never the final word about the way things are.

Economic theory, however, can be helpful in that it tells us what to expect if the hypotheses are true. The discussion in Chapter 6 is an example of such a use. Here we are asking what effect an upward shifting consumption function would have on the long-run growth of the economy.

The upward shifting function was characterized by the following equation:

$$C_t = (A_{\mathrm{III}} + Dt) + bY_t$$

At this point, let t be measured in years instead of months, so that the consumption schedule shifts up by an amount D every year. According to the elementary form of the theory of income determination, the equilibrium level shifts up by $D/(1 - b)$ every year if the level of investment is not changing. If the capital-output ratio is a constant denoted by v, then investment of $vD/(1 - b)$ will increase capacity by the same amount that the equilibrium output is increasing every year.

By means of illustration consider the following example, which has been carefully constructed so that difficulties of coordinating investment and consumption decisions do not arise. Suppose that the consumption function is:

$$C_t = (1080 + 120t) + .8Y_t$$

Let initial capacity output be 12,000. The consumption function shifts up 120 every year. With a marginal propensity to consume of .8, the multiplier is 5 and the equilibrium level will shift up by 600 every year ($D/(1 - b) = 600$). With a capital-output ratio of 2 ($v = 2$), net investment must be 1200 every year in order to increase capacity to produce by 600. Thus, with $I_1 = 1200$ and $A_1 = 1080 + 120$ in equation (7.4), the equilibrium level of net national product in year 1 is:

$$\bar{Y}_1 = \frac{(1080 + 120) + 1200}{.2} = \frac{2400}{.2} = 12,000$$

Capacity for year 2 then rises to 12,600. If investment stays at 1200 and the consumption function shifts up by 120, then the equilibrium for year 2 is equal to the capacity of 12,600:

$$\bar{Y}_2 = \frac{(1080 + 240) + 1200}{.2} = \frac{2520}{.2} = 12,600$$

This process can continue indefinitely with output growing linearly by 600 every year without any increase in net investment. Instead of a stationary state, we have an *equilibrium path* in which plans and expectations can be fulfilled period after period. An equilibrium path is like a stationary state in that aggregate supply equals aggregate demand and producers continue doing the same things each period, except that the "same things" include adding to capacity and steadily increasing production.

There is still the possibility of business cycles, of ups and downs in the level of business activity in a system like this; but the cycles will take place around an upward trend. The growth in the aggregate demand schedule does not eliminate the possibility of cycles, and may even aggravate them; but the high and low points of successive cycles will occur at higher levels.

If the consumption function shifts upward at some geometric rate (such as 5 percent per year), then NNP along the equilibrium path can be shown to grow geometrically (instead of linearly as in the preceding example) and investment would have to grow at the same geometric rate. In that case, investment, along the equilibrium path, would always be a constant proportion of net national product. The point is that there is no "general" theory of growth. Furthermore, government policies (discussed in Chapter 8) may have a direct bearing on the extent of economic growth, particularly in the short run.

9 U.S. EXPERIENCE, 1929–1968

Some data from the U.S. economy can now be interpreted. Figure 7.3 presents a panoramic view of GNP and investment for the period 1929 to 1968. At the top of the figure is a plot of real (constant dollar) GNP. The Great Depression can be seen in the substantial drop in GNP through 1933, a mild recovery, and a slight drop from 1937. By 1939 GNP was still at about the 1929 level. The huge rise of GNP in the early forties is attributable to World War II. Reconversion from wartime to peacetime production caused the postwar drop in 1945 and most notably in 1946. The years since World War II have been characterized by general growth interrupted by a series of recessions. These recessions occurred in 1949, 1953–1954, 1957–1958, and to a lesser extent in 1960–1961. The annual data do not show these recessions as clearly as do data over shorter intervals, but there is evidence of dips in the annual GNP in 1949, 1954, and 1958, and a slowing in the rate of growth around 1960. From 1961 to 1968 the U.S. economy has evidenced a remarkably strong boom.

A relationship between investment and GNP can also be seen in Figure 7.3, where both fixed investment and investment in inventories have been plotted. As the Great Depression gathered momentum fixed investment continued to fall and undoubtedly shifted down the temporary equilibrium that the economy was seeking. There was also a substantial liquidation of business inventories, seen as negative inventory investment. A similar pattern occurs in the 1938 dip. Fixed investment fell and inventory investment became negative.

The huge rise in GNP during World War II does not accompany an increase in investment. In fact investment fell. Most of the increase in aggregate demand was caused by an upsurge in government demand to sustain the war effort. The postwar recessions have often been characterized as inventory recessions. In Figure 7.3, the recession years — 1949, 1954, and 1958 — can be seen to have substantial dips in the inventory investment series. Fixed investment also fell in 1949 and 1958. In an effort to cut inventories many businesses cut production. As in the classroom economy, this apparently influences aggregate demand. Finally, the strong boom from 1961 to 1968 was reinforced by growing levels of planned investment.

There is one more aspect to the U.S. experience to be examined here: the extent of price changes over the period 1929–1968. In Figure 7.4 are plotted the series for both the wholesale price index and the consumer price index. The wholesale price index provides a measure of the extent of price changes on large lots that manufacturers sell to other manufacturers, distributors, and retailers. The consumer price index measures the price changes that have taken place in the bundle of goods and services that the typical consumer is likely to buy. The data are prepared by the U.S. Bureau of Labor Statistics and are available monthly. Figure 7.4 shows the annual averages. With a few exceptions the two series appear to move together. The biggest increases in prices have occurred when there have been the biggest upsurges in aggregate demand with the economy already close to full capacity. The largest jumps occurred during and right after World War II. In fact, so great was the inflationary pressure during the war that rationing and price controls were instituted. With the war-created shortage of goods, a large accumulation of personal savings, and the end of price control, there was a strong surge in prices until the recession of 1949. The beginning of the Korean War in the middle of 1950 led to further price increases, followed by a few years of relatively stable prices. The price increases in the period 1956–1958 do not fit the usual pattern in that this period includes a recession in economic activity. From 1958 into the early

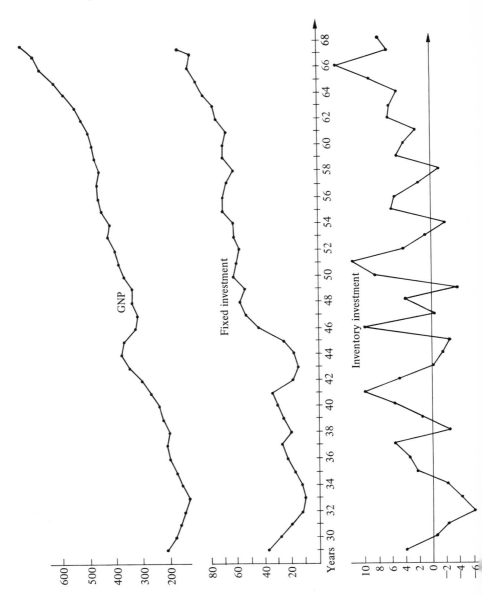

Figure 7.3 **GNP, Fixed Investment, and Inventory Investment in Constant (1958) Dollars for the U.S. Economy, 1929–1968**

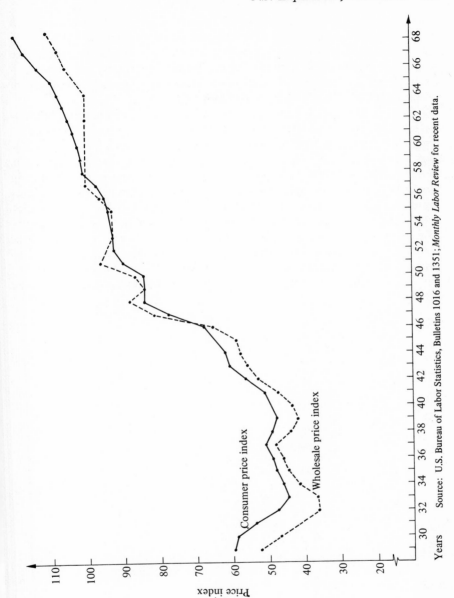

Figure 7.4   Indexes of Prices in the U.S. Economy, 1929–1968

sixties, when GNP was growing only moderately and the economy had plenty of excess capacity, the wholesale price index was remarkably steady while the consumer price index moved up moderately, primarily because of the increasing cost of services. Again the strong demand accompanying a war effort, this time the Vietnam War, resulted in upward pressures on prices from 1965 and continuing through 1968.

This look at the U.S. experience has been in terms of broad aggregates. Nevertheless, the analysis in this chapter appears relevant to facts of experience. Steady growth has by no means been easy to achieve and maintain. The Great Depression was largely the result of inadequate aggregate demand. The upward shifts of the aggregate demand schedule during World War II demonstrated the economy's potential as did the stimulants applied to the economy in the 1960s (to be discussed in the next chapter). Fixed investment has been fairly volatile although not so much as the discussion in conjunction with the classroom economy might suggest. The fact that inventory investment goes from periods of accumulation to periods of decumulation certainly indicates that U.S. businesses (and not just firms in the classroom economy) periodically adjust their inventory positions.

8

GOVERNMENT FISCAL POLICIES

According to the national income and product accounts for the U.S. economy in 1967, government purchases of goods and services constitute about 22 percent of the gross national product, and government transfer payments are an important part of disposable personal income. Moreover, the nature of government taxing and spending decisions can have an influence on economic activity. It is desirable, therefore, to incorporate government decisions into the theory of income determination.

1 FISCAL POLICY

The term *fiscal policy* will refer to decisions by governments to spend and to tax. The actual policy may be the result of a series of haphazard and uncoordinated decisions, or the decisions may all be part of a well-articulated plan. If there is a plan, it may be motivated by political considerations, or it may seek to influence the economy. Whether fiscal policy is or is not coordinated, the decisions by governments do influence the economy. A decision not to change taxes can be just as monumental as one to make a change. Questions of how to tax and whom to tax come under the category of public finance and are problems in the management of government, but they are also a part of fiscal policy decisions. Questions of how to allocate government spending — how much for poverty programs, highways, veterans' benefits, armaments, space exploration, education, and

119

so on — are important aspects of fiscal policy. Such decisions vitally affect the utilization of resources within an economy. In a book on macroeconomics, however, the focus is on the total amount of government expenditures and receipts. This should not be construed as a denial of the importance of the composition of government expenditures and taxation. But the concept of fiscal policy emphasizes the importance of these totals in their own right.

In 1946 the U.S. Congress passed what is now known as the Employment Act of 1946. Following the Great Depression of the 1930s and the upheaval of World War II, this act states that "it is the continuing policy and responsibility of the Federal Government . . . to promote maximum employment, production, and purchasing power." There are numerous qualifications stated in the act, but the main point is that the Federal Government has declared its responsibility for keeping income and employment high. Among other things the act established the Council of Economic Advisors to assist and advise the President in the preparation of the Economic Report of the President, which appears every January, and in general to make studies and recommendations on matters of economic policy at the request of the President. How some aspects of macroeconomic theory have been used in furthering the aims of the Employment Act of 1946 will be considered in this chapter.

2   GOVERNMENT AND AGGREGATE DEMAND

Government purchases of goods and services can be treated as a form of consumption expenditures, except that they are made collectively by government agencies. These expenditures should be shown explicitly in the theory of income determination, however, since they are determined in accordance with policy objectives and not by rules of behavior postulated for the household sector.

Aggregate demand for goods and services includes demand for consumer goods by households and for planned net investment by business. These have been discussed in earlier chapters. Now the demand for goods and services by governments is also recognized as being a part of aggregate demand. If G stands for planned government purchases, then aggregate demand can be written $C + I + G$, and the equilibrium condition that aggregate supply equal aggregate demand becomes:

$$Y = C + I + G. \tag{8.1}$$

The consumption function hypothesis must also be restated. Economists generally accept the notion that consumption is a function primarily of disposable income and an exercise in Chapter 6 asked the class to examine this relationship. The hypothesis is that consumers decide how much to buy by looking at their income after taxes rather than at their total income. Taxes, transfer payments, and corporate retained earnings create a discrepancy between NNP and disposable income. If these items are negligible, then consumption will be approximately the same function of NNP that it is of disposable income. In the U.S. economy, however, these items are not negligible. The figures in Tables 4.1 and 4.2 attest to this fact. In 1967, income taxes (personal and corporate) plus corporate retained earnings totaling $181.9 billion were included in national income but not in disposable income. $75.3 billion were returned to the household sector via transfer payments, leaving a net drain of $106.6 billion. There is also a figure of $67.6 billion in indirect business taxes less some minor adjustments included in net national product but not in national income or disposable income. This means that disposable income was about $174 billion less than net national product in 1967. This difference between net national product and disposable income will be called *net taxes* and will be denoted by the symbol T.[1]

If consumption is a function of disposable income, the general linear consumption function can be written:

$$C = A + c (Y - T) \qquad (8.2)$$

where c is the marginal propensity to consume out of disposable income.

Taxes are usually levied on the basis of rates. For example, sales taxes are stated as a rate, such as 4 percent of the dollar value of items sold, and income-tax schedules show rates that must be paid on different levels of income. This suggests that taxes will vary with the level of economic activity. Evidence confirms that a relationship does exist.

Table 8.1 shows NNP and personal disposable income over the last few years. The difference between these two magnitudes has been called net taxes, which is shown in column (3). Net taxes have been fairly close to 24 per cent of NNP over these years. See column (4). This suggests the following hypothesis:

$$T = rY \qquad (8.3)$$

Call r the tax rate, even though there are numerous factors that influence the relationship between T and Y. However, since any legislation that alters

---

[1]Net taxes, as defined here, includes corporate retained earnings (a form of business taxation of stockholders). If we wished to analyze retained earnings and government revenues separately, it would be necessary to introduce separate categories into our equations.

Table 8.1

Year	(1) Net national product	(2) Disposable personal income	(3) T (1) − (2)	(4) T/NNP (3) ÷ (1)	(5) Retained earnings
1967	720.5	546.3	174.2	.242	23.1
1966	679.8	508.8	171.0	.251	27.5
1965	624.0	472.2	151.8	.243	25.4
1964	576.3	438.1	138.2	.240	20.6
1963	537.9	404.6	133.3	.248	16.6
1962	510.4	385.3	125.0	.245	16.0
1961	474.9	364.4	110.5	.233	13.5
1960	460.3	350.0	110.3	.240	13.2
1959	442.3	337.3	105.0	.237	15.9

Source: *Survey of Current Business*, July 1968, July 1967, and August 1965.

tax schedules will affect r, we shall proceed as if r can be manipulated directly.[2]

If rY is substituted for T in consumption function (8.2), then consumption as a function of NNP becomes:

$$C = A + c(1 - r)Y \tag{8.4}$$

To obtain the equilibrium NNP, substitute this form of the consumption function into equilibrium condition (8.1):

$$Y = A + c(1 - r)Y + I + G$$

and solve for Y:

$$\bar{Y} = \frac{A + I + G}{1 - c(1 - r)} = \frac{A + I + G}{1 - b} \tag{8.5}$$

Compare the consumption function (8.4) with the function (5.4) introduced in Chapter 5. The only difference is that the parameter b, the marginal propensity to consume out of net national product, has now been written as the product of two terms: $(1 - r)$, the proportion of net national product that becomes disposable income, and c, the marginal propensity to consume out of disposable income. Written in this latter manner, the expression can be used to show the effects of changes in the rate r, but otherwise there is

[2]It appears that the ratio T/Y tends to grow as the economy expands rapidly, reflecting in part the progressive structure of the tax schedules and in part the fact that corporate dividends do not change as rapidly as corporate profits. Column (5) of Table 8.1 shows business retained earnings. Clearly, the ratio T/NNP is moderately sensitive to business decisions about how much of their earnings to pay out in dividends.

still the same sort of hypothesized relationship between net national product and consumer demand.

Equation (8.5) indicates that the equilibrium level of net national product may be influenced not only by consumer decisions, represented by the values of A and c, and by business investment decisions I, but also by government fiscal policy decisions which are reflected in the values of G and r.

As an example, let:

$$A = 0$$
$$I = 35.5$$
$$G = 125.0$$
$$c = 0.93$$
$$r = 0.248$$

Some of these numbers may seem unduly complicated for an illustrative example. They have not been selected arbitrarily, however. In 1963 the Council of Economic Advisors indicated its guesses on the numerical values of these coefficients. It is therefore useful to take these as approximations to an opinion that was once officially held. (Usually the Council does not express its views in a form so useful for teaching purposes.)

One simplification of this example will be made by rounding off the MPC out of net national product:

$$b = c(1 - r) = .93(.752) = .70$$

The consumption function can then be written:

$$C = .70\ Y$$

and from equation (8.5) the equilibrium level of NNP will be:

$$\bar{Y} = \frac{35.5 + 125.0}{1 - .70} = \frac{160.5}{.3} = 535$$

This result is shown graphically in Figure 8.1. Aggregate demand has been built up in stages. First consumption has been drawn as a function of net national product and labeled C. Then planned investment of 35.5 has been added to consumption at each level of Y. This combination is labelled $C + I$. Finally the government demand of 125 has been added to depict aggregate demand as a function of Y. Only when aggregate supply is 535 does aggregate demand equal aggregate supply. When Y is above 535, supply exceeds demand and is likely to fall. When Y is below 535, demand exceeds supply and Y is likely to rise.

This equilibrium level is to be treated as a temporary equilibrium that may or may not be reached before it changes. All it says is that if taxes, government purchases, planned investment, and the consumption function remain constant, then there is a level of net national product (535 in the example) at which all plans to buy and expectations of sales are fulfilled.

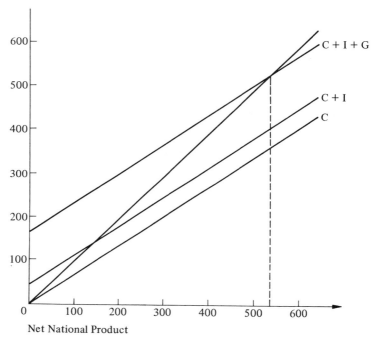

Figure 8.1 Equilibrium Net National Product with Government Expenditures

3 GOVERNMENT MULTIPLIERS

The multiplier has been defined in Chapter 5 as a ratio of the change in the equilibrium level of NNP to a shift in some flow parameter. In two previous encounters with this notion, the initiating shift has been either a change in the A-term of the consumption function or a change in planned investment. With the present formulation there are two more possible initiating shifts: (1) when government purchases change and (2) when net taxes change.

The shift in the equilibrium level of net national product is, as before, $1/(1 - b)$ times any shift in A or I. In the present example, b is equal to .70 and so the multiplier is $1/0.3$ or 3 and 1/3. If planned investment were to increase by 6, then the equilibrium Y would increase by 20.

The *government expenditures multiplier* is the ratio of the change in equilibrium net national product to the change in the value of G. If, in the example, G were to increase by 6, the effect is to increase equilibrium Y by 20. This can be verified by changing the value of G to 131 in the example and working out the resulting value of $\bar{Y}$. Thus, the multiplier effects of changes in A, I, or G, each taken separately are all the same.

When government fiscal policies are being considered, there is often concern about how a change in government spending or in the tax rates will alter the government budget surplus, which is equal to tax revenues minus government expenditures both for goods and services and for transfer payments. For analytical purposes, business retained earnings will be ignored and the difference $T - G$ will be treated as the government budget surplus. When T is greater than G, there is a budget surplus; and when G is greater than T there is a budget deficit.

Since recent debates about appropriate fiscal policy usually involve concern about the size of the government deficit and about how much a proposed policy might increase or decrease the deficit, we shall let D denote the government deficit and be equal to the value $G - T$.' A change in the deficit may arise from any number of changes in spending plans within the economy. At this point changes that arise either through revised tax schedules or a change in government expenditures are of primary interest. To indicate the initiating shift, a subscript will be appended to the symbol ΔD used to denote a change in the deficit. Thus:

$$\Delta D_G = \text{change in the deficit as a result of a change}$$
$$\text{in government spending.}$$

$$\Delta D_T = \text{change in the deficit as a result of a}$$
$$\text{change in taxes.}$$

If G is increased and the economy moves to its higher equilibrium level, net taxes also increase by r times the change in Y. If Y increases by 20 when G increases by 6, and the value of r is .248, then net taxes T will increase by almost 5. The net change in the deficit (change in G minus change in T) is only slightly greater than 1 and the ratio between the change in the equilibrium level of Y and the net change in the deficit is almost 20 to 1 when the expansion is initiated by government spending changes.

What happens to equilibrium net national product when net taxes change? Since net taxes are determined by both tax rates and the level of economic activity, the question must be answered in stages. Suppose the tax rate r were lowered to .237 in the example. In this case:

$$b = c\,(1 - r) = .93\,(.763) = .71$$

The new equilibrium level of Y is then:

$$\bar{Y} = \frac{160.5}{.29} = 553.4$$

This is 18.4 above the old equilibrium, illustrating the expansionary potential of a tax cut.

These relationships can be shown more explicitly in algebraic form. The formulas that require a moderate amount of manipulation to obtain are derived in the appendix to this chapter. The simpler derivations are shown in the next few pages. As notation, let

$r =$ the initial tax rate
$r' =$ the new tax rate
$\Delta G =$ change in the government expenditures
$\Delta T =$ change in net taxes
$Y =$ initial equilibrium level of net national product
$Y' =$ new equilibrium level of net national product

$$\Delta Y = Y' - Y \tag{8.6}$$

From the discussion of the government expenditures multiplier, we know that

$$\Delta Y = \frac{\Delta G}{1 - c + cr} \tag{8.7}$$

when there is no change in r. At the same time net taxes will rise by r times the change in Y, that is,

$$\Delta T = \frac{r\Delta G}{1 - c + cr}$$

Consequently the change in the government deficit becomes:

$$\Delta D_G = \Delta G - \Delta T$$
$$= \frac{(1 - c + cr)\,\Delta G - r\Delta G}{1 - c + cr}$$
$$= \frac{(1 - c)\,(1 - r)\,\Delta G}{1 - c + cr}$$

The ratio of the change in Y to the change in the deficit is therefore

$$\frac{\Delta Y}{\Delta D_G} = \frac{1/(1 - c + cr)}{(1 - c)\,(1 - r)/(1 - c + cr)}$$

or $$\frac{\Delta Y}{\Delta D_G} = \frac{1}{(1 - c)\,(1 - r)} \tag{8.8}$$

as a result of new government spending. In the example with $c = .93$ and $r = .248$:

$$\frac{\Delta Y}{\Delta D_G} = \frac{1}{(.07)\,(.752)} = 19.0$$

This particular number should not be taken too seriously. It does suggest that a change in the government deficit initiated by a change in government spending can have a substantial effect on the equilibrium NNP, assuming other things the same. But other influences, notably actions by monetary authorities, which have not been explicitly incorporated into this introductory treatment of macroeconomic theory, may have either intensifying or offsetting impacts. In other words, the assumption that other things remain unchanged is of great importance in our illustrative estimate of this government deficit multiplier.

A slightly more involved derivation, presented in the appendix, shows that the expansionary effect on net national product from a change in the deficit initiated by a tax change is:

$$\frac{\Delta Y}{\Delta D_T} = \frac{c}{1 - c} \tag{8.9}$$

In the example, with $c = .93$,

$$\frac{c}{1 - c} = \frac{.93}{.07} = 13.3.$$

The remarks accompanying the preceding deficit multiplier are also relevant here.

Before going on, consider the question whether or not net taxes can be higher after a tax cut than before. In other words, could the change in Y induce a sufficiently great increase in taxes to offset the lower rate with the result that ΔT might be positive? The answer, demonstrated in the appendix, is no. *Unless there is some increase in* A, I, G, *or* c, *net taxes* T *must be lower as the result of a cut in tax rates* even though the equilibrium level of income is higher.

Another question of interest is the extent to which a change in the deficit as the result of changing government expenditures is more expansionary than that initiated through tax changes. Compare expressions (8.8) and (8.9). The ratio of the latter, the tax effect, to the former, the expenditure effect, is:

$$\frac{c/(1 - c)}{1/(1 - c)(1 - r)} = c\,(1 - r) = b$$

This result is to be interpreted as follows. A dollar added to the government deficit through tax changes is only b times as potent in stimulating the economy as a dollar deficit resulting from expenditure changes. b

is the marginal propensity to consume out of net national product and is equal to .70 in the example. One can readily verify that the ratio of the two deficit multipliers 13.3 and 19.0 is 0.70.

One final multiplier will be considered. It is known as the *balanced budget multiplier* and arises in answer to the following question: What is the effect on equilibrium net national product if both government expenditures and tax revenues rise by the same amount? In other words, what happens when there is a balanced increase in both G and T? With no change in A, I, or c, the answer is that equilibrium Y rises by the same amount as the increase in government expenditures. This is shown in the appendix.

This is an interesting result. It means that the government can exert an expansionary effect on the economy by increasing the level of its expenditures even if every additional dollar expended is matched by additional tax collections; and going the other way, a balanced budget decrease has a contractionary effect.

Comparing the new equilibrium position after a balanced budget change in government purchases with the earlier equilibrium discloses a fascinating result. Disposable income is unchanged, since net taxes and net national product have both increased by the same amount. With the same level of disposable income and an unchanged consumption function, consumers are buying just as much as before. Net investment has been assumed not to change. As a result, the government can increase its purchases of goods and services with no loss to the consumers or to business investment plans, *if there are sufficient idle resources* and if no other effects come into play. If the economy were operating at close to full capacity, such an increase in government's share of total product could drive up prices and leave private buyers of consumer and investment goods with less product in real terms; but with excess capacity in the economy, government can utilize resources that might otherwise have been wasted without sacrificing other economic interests and without incurring any new budget deficit.

This conclusion should bother some readers. We are saying that when governments tax individuals and use the revenue to pay workers to perform services, the private sector's income after taxes rises (in equilibrium) by the amount that governments have paid to these workers. In effect these services have not cost anybody anything, and if the services are useful, so much the better. If there are idle resources and if the economy moves from one equilibrium to another, this conclusion is the direct result of the assumptions used and as such is incontrovertible once the assumptions are accepted.

One of the assumptions that appears most implausible is that planned investment by the business sector is not affected by the nature or magnitude of any government tax or expenditure changes. As illustrated in Section 4 of this chapter, fiscal policy proposals do take some account of possible influences on planned investment. The exercise suggested for the class in Section 6 requires consideration of hypothetical government actions on investment decisions in the classroom economy.

4 MANIPULATING U.S. TAX RATES

In recent years there have cases in which tax laws were changed for reasons explicitly related to the level of economic activity. One of the more interesting events in terms of the theory presented in this book occurred in 1964. In February of 1964 Congress passed and the President signed into law the Revenue Act of 1964. The act revised downward the tax rates on personal and corporate income for the expressed purpose of stimulating the economy. The cut in taxes that took effect partly in 1964 and partly in 1965 was estimated to be about $11.5 billion based on 1963 income levels. The example presented above was taken from testimony in favor of this piece of legislation before its enactment. Extensive discussion is to be found in the *Hearings on the Revenue Act of 1963* before the Committee on Finance of the U.S. Senate (to be referred to here as *Hearings*).

By late 1963, the U.S. economy had been advancing steadily since a recession low in February 1961. Nevertheless, unemployment remained close to 6.0 percent instead of the 4 percent of the labor force that was considered to be a tolerable level of unemployment without generating serious inflationary pressures. Manufacturers on the average were producing at close to 85 percent of capacity when 92 percent was considered about optimal.[3] It followed that there was an unused potential for production of goods and services within the U.S. economy. Furthermore, projections showed that a substantial growth in the labor force could be expected in the next few years.

It was proposed to reduce personal income taxes by $8.8 billion and corporate income taxes by about $2.2 billion. The testimony of Walter Heller, then chairman of President John F. Kennedy's Council of Economic Advisors, indicates how he expected the proposed cut to affect the economy (*Hearings*, p. 1583). Approximately $1 billion of the corporate tax cut was expected to be passed on to individuals through increased dividends. This, together with the cut in personal income taxes, would increase disposable income by close to $10 billion. Since, it was claimed, consumers always spend

[3]In the U.S. economy, capacity is not so easily defined as it was in the classroom economy. Firms often have standby equipment and can add extra labor (when available) to increase output if they so choose, but these short-run adjustments usually increase average costs of production. The potential is there if prices and quantity demanded justify greater production. In the long-run there are more efficient ways of meeting the higher demand if it persists. Therefore, some excess capacity is desired for purposes of short-run flexibility.

about 93 percent of their disposable income, the projected $10 billion increase in disposable income was expected to shift consumption up by at least $9 billion. The cut in corporate income taxes plus the stimulus provided by higher demand was expected also to induce an added $6 billion in planned investment by business. Combined, these represent an upward shift of $15 billion in the aggregate demand schedule. Using a multiplier figure of 2, Heller claimed that this would raise GNP by $30 billion, thus increasing both employment and utilization of manufacturers' plant capacity. The alternative, it was feared, would be a business downturn by 1964 or perhaps 1965 if the tax cut was not enacted.

From our analytical discussion, it may seem strange that a multiplier of only 2 would be applied when consumers were expected to spend over 90 percent of their increased disposable income. The example above, in which $c = .93$, was based on Heller's testimony. Undoubtedly he was being intentionally cautious in his presentation. This is one way to allow for unforeseen offsetting events. The important point is that the gist of the argument presented to the U.S. Senators comes straight from the elementary theory of income determination.

In 1963 NNP was about 535 (dropping the references to dollars and billions and rounding off the actual figures a bit). Seventy percent of this is about 375, approximately the level of consumption expenditures in that year. Suppose planned net investment was 35.5 and government purchases of goods and services were 125 (also close to the reported figures for investment and government). We thus hypothesize that the economy was approximately in its temporary equilibrium since $\bar{Y} = 535$ was the result obtained above when $A = 0$, $c(1 - r) = .7$, $I = 35.5$, and $G = 125$.

Now suppose that the tax cut lowers r from .248 to .237. When $Y = 535$ with r lower by .011, the initial decrease in net taxes is almost 6, slightly over half of the proposed cut. If there is no change in planned investment, our example above suggests that equilibrium income will rise by over 18. If planned investment were to increase by 6, the new temporary equilibrium is:

$$\bar{Y} = \frac{166.5}{.29} = 574$$

for an increase of almost 40 over the assumed 1963 level of Y.

Whatever the appropriate figure might have been for the effect of the tax cut on production and employment, what bothered many senators was the idea of deliberately increasing the deficit of the Federal Government in a time of relative prosperity. Without debating the rationale for such a concern, we can say that the answers by the proponents of the bill were never fully satisfactory to these senators. Take the projected increase in GNP of $30 billion and note that Federal tax revenues were close to 20 percent of GNP in 1963 (*Hearings*, p. 1582), Federal tax revenue would increase by

20 percent of $30 billion, that is, by $6 billion after the new equilibrium was reached following the tax cut of $11 billion. Therefore, while output and employment could be stimulated by the tax cut, it did appear that the net effect of the tax cut alone would be to add about $5 billion to the Federal Government's deficit.

To see how this question was answered, consider the testimony of Douglas Dillon, Secretary of the Treasury (*Hearings*, p. 124). "The tax base rises and falls with economic activity. The economic expansion we can expect from passage of this tax cut bill will thus 'feed back' increased tax revenues sufficient to achieve a balanced budget at substantially reduced tax rates, provided expenditures are restrained."

It has been pointed out above and demonstrated in the appendix of this chapter that with the assumptions employed in analyzing the probable impact of a tax cut alone, there must be an increase in the government deficit.[4] Under questioning by the Senators, Dillon disclosed how he expected the tax cut to result in a balanced budget. The reasoning was pieced together and presented by Professor Richard Musgrave, an economist, who appeared before the committee about eight weeks later. Balance could be achieved by 1968 if the government's receipts were to grow by a "normal" amount of $6 billion per year from 1966 through 1968 and government expenditures were to grow by $2.5 billion per year.

What is missing in the argument is any explicit statement of the mechanism that would sustain an upward shifting equilibrium. If the economy was in equilibrium in 1963 and were to move to the new temporary equilibrium after the tax cut, what would provide the further impetus to keep tax revenues rising by $6 billion per year? In Heller's testimony the consumption function (8.4) has been formulated in such a way that upward shifts appear to be ruled out. His consumption function contains no A-term. If there is no shift in the consumption function, an upward shifting equilibrium might occur because of an accelerator effect: business investment plans rise in response to increases in the national product; but if we believe the figures given to Congress, planned investment must then rise beyond the $6 billion increase postulated by Heller as a direct effect of the proposed tax cut if continued growth in NNP is to take place.

Another possibility that could provide an upward shifting equilibrium would be further tax cuts or greater increases in government expenditures. This, however, could add to the government deficit and would be inconsistent with the projections given to Congress for government expenditures and tax receipts beyond 1965.

In effect, the government economists were assuming that the economy

[4]In our example, an upward shift of 6 in planned net investment would be sufficient to decrease the government deficit, but this is not the case in the figures actually given to Congress.

readily moves from one temporary equilibrium to another. Rather than specifying what might determine continuing upward shifts, they appeared willing to formulate fiscal policy in terms of an explicit short-run hypothesis and a fuzzy statement about the probable longer-run process.

As events unfolded after the tax cut of 1964, the stimulants to the economy proved greater than had been predicted. Net investment rose by almost $10 billion from 1964 to 1965. Some excise taxes were cut in 1965, and the American military involvement in Vietnam resulted in greatly expanded government expenditures. In 1966 aggregate demand rose still higher as government spending continued to mount. The temporary equilibrium was undoubtedly above the economy's capacity to produce, for prices began rising faster than they had in the early 1960s. By 1966 the government was seeking measures to curb aggregate demand so as to slow down the rise in prices.

In his Economic Report in 1967 and more emphatically in 1968, the President requested Congress to enact an income-tax surcharge. This is a tax on a tax. If a man owes $1000 in taxes on the basis of existing tax schedules and the surcharge is 10 percent then he will pay an additional $100 in taxes. Battle lines were drawn over this proposed tax increase. A few Congressmen had doubts about its necessity, but the strongest opposition came from those who wanted major spending cuts. To some extent they used the argument from macroeconomic theory that a spending cut is more potent in its impact than a tax increase, but the prime thrust was more a distrust or dislike of large government outlays. Legislators supported or opposed spending cuts, depending on whether or not they opposed the programs in question, considered in isolation. Thus, their motives were of a political nature (which is not to call them evil) and were not based on considerations of macroeconomic theory.

Unlike the arguments used by the administration in 1963 when the effect of the proposed tax cut on the deficit was treated as a minor issue, the arguments of the administration in 1967 and 1968 for the tax increase often pointed to the desirability of decreasing the huge deficit. This, of course, could be accomplished by a spending reduction too. At issue was not whether fiscal policy should be used to exert a restraining influence on aggregate demand but rather whether government spending should be cut or private spending should be restrained by higher taxes.

The outcome was a compromise. Toward the end of June 1968, the Revenue Expenditure Control Act of 1968 cleared Congress and was signed into law by the President. It provided for a 10 percent surcharge on personal and corporate income taxes to run until June of 1969. In addition, with some exemptions, Congress set a ceiling on federal spending that was $6 billion below the spending estimates in the Budget. Furthermore, it required the President to submit plans in fiscal year 1970 for an additional $8 billion cut in unspent prior-year appropriations. Thus, there were spending cuts and a tax increase.

For the student who wishes to get quick summaries of actions taken by Congress and the positions of individual Senators and Representatives, a good source is the Congressional Quarterly's *Weekly Reports.* The hearings before committees considering legislation usually provide detailed arguments by both proponents and opponents of a bill. For a summary of Federal fiscal policies in the 1960s, see the *Federal Reserve Bulletin,* September 1968. Our brief considerations of two pieces of legislation suggest that macroeconomic theory does play at least a part in decisions involving federal taxing and spending programs.

5 THE PROBLEM OF TIMING

There are serious problems about the timing as well as the magnitude of government fiscal policies, since there are lags in recognition, decision, execution, and impact. Take a recession as an example. At any time during an expansion, there may be warning signals of an impending downturn such as a slowing in the rate of growth in the economy, an upturn in unemployment, a number of industries recording declining sales. In judging whether or not a recession is imminent, an observer must sort out temporary aberrations in an expanding economy from signs of the beginning of a general downturn. Because economic data are not available until some time after events have occurred and because it is hard to tell whether or not a recession is beginning, the economy may be a few months into a recession before most analysts are convinced of the fact.

Once the seriousness of the economy's ills has been diagnosed, there is the question of the appropriate cure. Suppose it is generally agreed that the Congress should act to reverse the downturn. In recent years the President has taken the initiative in proposing fiscal policy changes, presumably on the advice of his economic advisors. Congress will want to take a few months, and maybe years, to evaluate and deliberate any proposal, whether it be for a tax cut, an increase in Federal appropriations and authorizations for spending, or for some stimulant to business investment expenditures. Thus more months may pass before Congress acts (or fails to act) on the proposal.

Finally there may be a further lag in implementing and realizing the impact of the action. In some cases, the initial impact may come fairly quickly as in the case of government expenditures that involve procurement from private manufacturers with excess capacity. As soon as a contract is let, the manufacturer may begin hiring, placing orders for supplies and subcontracting part of the work. In this case, the increase in aggregate demand may take place well before the government actually makes its payments. In the case of a tax cut, the speed of the impact depends on the reactions in the household sector. If initially people tend to save a large portion of the increase in disposable income (as happened for a few months after the tax cut in 1964) and only later begin to increase their expenditures for consumer goods, there can be delayed impact. In the case of stimulants to business investment, many investment plans require long-range commitments that are unlikely to be changed quickly. The corporate managers may wait to see what effect changes in the law have upon their company's financial position before they undertake investment to modernize or expand their plant facilities. The extent of such lags poses another research problem for economists.

This chapter, so far, has ignored the adjustment process itself. The economy has been assumed to jump readily from one equilibrium to another so that it is always in or close to equilibrium. If the economy is rarely in equilibrium and takes a long time to move toward its equilibrium level, the appropriateness of various policy measures becomes even more difficult to assess. Decisions taken to combat a recession may aggravate subsequent inflationary pressures, and measures to stem inflation may result somewhat later in worsening a recession. Chapter 9 contains additional comments about this possibility.

Economists are increasingly involved in the formulation of governmental policies. If they can maintain a healthy perspective and alter their recommendations as economic conditions change, they are useful to governments. Economists, if they have a public forum, can and do influence people's evaluations of what is a desirable or undesirable course of action. For example, with a careful analysis an economist may be able to provide a quantitative estimate of the costs and benefits from a proposed government project. He can say which alternative actions might achieve given objectives such as getting unemployment from 6 percent to 4 percent of the labor force or holding inflation to a moderate amount while supporting a war effort. The correctness of his estimates of the costs, benefits, and probable impacts of various policy measures depends on the behavioral assumptions on which the analysis rests. As we have emphasized, particularly in Chapter 6, the exact response of consumers or businesses to changes in economic conditions can rarely be estimated precisely; but economists, being specialists in these questions, are apt to do better than others in providing answers.

6 AN EXERCISE IN FISCAL POLICY

To illustrate the difficulty in making appropriate policy decisions, we return to the classroom economy, not because this is the way things are likely to be in a real economy but because it is simple enough for the students, at this point, to have a reasonably good understanding of how it works. There are no external events to take into account and a great deal is known about the behavior of the key decision-makers within the economy. By now, the students undoubtedly have a good estimate of the consumption function used in their own classroom economy.

Before considering the problem, we should note the elements contained in any economic policy problem. There is an *agent* who must make decisions. Whatever variables are under his control are called *instruments*. The instruments of managers of firms in the classroom economy are orders of materials and levels of production. Nothing else is under their control. In the fiscal policy problem, the instruments will be the level of government spending and the tax rate.

There is also an *institutional setting*. This involves all aspects of the problem that are beyond the direct control of the agent. For example, the structure of the classroom economy characterizes the institutional setting for managers of firms in the classroom economy. A full specification of the institutional setting includes such items as the state of technology, the constraints imposed on the decision-making agent, and the behavior of other agents elsewhere in the economy. Some of the elements of the institutional setting are clearly specified. Other aspects require hypotheses about behavior of others.

Finally, there must be an *objective*, or set of goals, that the agent would like to achieve. If the objective, the institutional setting and the instruments are precisely stated, the appropriate policy is to choose those values of the instruments that best satisfy the objective. An inability to solve such a problem may arise because the objective is not clearly stated or because one does not know how to solve such a problem, but most often the difficulty stems from imprecise notions about the institutional setting, particularly with regard to the behavior of those whose actions are beyond the direct control of the agent. Managers in the classroom economy probably found that their greatest difficulty came in trying to assess what other managers were going to do. The same sort of problem confronts the government policy maker.

Suppose there is an individual or a committee of individuals who must make fiscal policy decisions for a classroom economy. They become the agent. Their instruments will be a tax rate r and a level of government expenditures. Details on these instruments follow.

Let it be possible to impose a tax rate r on spendable income so that

$$T_t = r Z_t$$

Let the consumption function be of the form:

$$C_t^* = A_t + c (Z_t - T_t)$$

or, upon substitution for T_t:

$$C_t^* = A_t + c(1 - r)Z_t$$

The higher the tax rate r, the lower will be the marginal propensity to consume out of spendable income and the lower will be consumer demand at each level of income. To illustrate, let

$$A_t = 220$$

$$c = .75$$

$$r = .2$$

Consumption as a function of spendable income is then

$$C_t^* = 220 + .6Z_t$$

If spendable income were 1000, total taxes would be 200. With $Z_t = 1000$, consumer demand would be 970 without the tax and only 820 with the tax. At that level of income, the consumption function is evidently shifted down by 150 because of the tax or by 3/4 of the total tax revenue.

This is a way to generate revenue for a hypothetical government in the classroom economy and to depress consumer demand. On the expenditure side, the government might choose to buy investment goods as well as consumer goods. Suppose, however, that the government in the classroom economy buys only consumer goods and redistributes them as the decision makers in the government see fit. For the problem being posed it is convenient to assume that the government's allocation of its purchases does not alter the consumption function. (For a real economy one would not necessarily take this assumption as valid.)

With regard to the institutional setting, further restrictions will be introduced in order to make the problem interesting. For example, the government may not guarantee to buy all the consumer goods that consumers do not buy at the going market price. That possibility is too far removed from the way things happen in actual life (except for some farm-support programs) to be worth considering. Another possibility would be for the government to announce in advance its purchase plans. This would be something like the President's budget message to Congress in January or the passing of authorization and appropriation bills by the Congress. The difference is that in the United States every firm that eventually receives a government contract is not likely to acquire the materials and begin production until after the contract has been received, while in the classroom economy every firm would know precisely its share of the government business. Consequently, for the classroom exercise in fiscal policy, government demand should be lumped into announced potential sales so that the size of the government purchases are known only after the classroom income accounts become available.

To introduce a problem of forecasting into the government decisions, the level of G_{t+1} (government purchases in period $t + 1$) and the selected tax rate for period $t + 1$ should be recorded privately by the agent responsible for making these decisions as of the beginning of month t. This requires a two-month forecast in that information is available only through month $t - 1$ when G is determined for month $t + 1$. Government policy decisions would then have to anticipate what managers of firms and the consumers are going to do two months hence.

If such an experiment were carried out, the students who make the government decisions would have to submit their decisions to the teacher when the firms' decisions are submitted. In computing potential sales, the teacher would alter the marginal propensity to consume in accordance with the selected tax rate and add government expenditures to the A-term in the consumption function. The product side of the classroom income accounts would have to include government expenditures, and spendable income would be reported with taxes deducted from the before-tax level.

Suppose such a procedure had been introduced into the classroom economy at the beginning of month 3 with the tax rate and government spending to begin taking effect in month 4. What kind of decision rules would each student suggest that the government follow in formulating decisions? Before he can answer such a question, he would have to know what would be considered good results. In other words, an objective needs to be specified.

The fiscal policy decisions should work to get the economy to the point at which every firm is producing and selling exactly 100 units of output every period. (If this experiment is conducted, the capacity constraint of 100 units of output per period should be rigidly enforced.) Thus, one goal might be to have as little unused capacity as possible.

A second goal might be to avoid excess demand. If potential sales exceed the output of firms, we shall say that the extent of this difference is a measure of excess demand. Suppose that government demand is always met, so that when firms miss sales it is the household sector's demand that goes unsatisfied.

A third goal might be for the government to achieve a balanced budget in every period. A moment's reflection reveals that the achievement of one goal may mean the sacrificing of other goals. For example, if government purchases are set at a high level it may rapidly eliminate unused capacity at the expense of substantial excess demand and unbalanced budgets.

Without going into the relative merits of removing unused capacity, avoiding excess demand, and the maintenance of a balanced budget by the government, we shall for analytical purposes arbitrarily assign a penalty cost of one for every unit of consumer goods that is not produced but could have been produced at full capacity, a penalty cost of one for each unit of potential sales that is not sold, and a penalty cost of one for each unit of real NNP that government expenditures differ from government revenues (no matter which is the larger). These penalty costs are to be assigned in every period.

The objective can then be to minimize (make as small as possible) the sum of the penalty costs over the periods for which the fiscal policy experiment is conducted. Restated, the problem is to set the tax rate and the level of government spending two months in advance so as to make as small as possible the sum of all penalty costs. The solution to such a problem is by no means obvious for it depends on the reactions of both the household and the business sector to the government decisions, and there is no precise information about how they will behave, particularly in the business sector of the classroom economy.

Furthermore, the appropriate policy (if it can be found) depends on the objective. If instead of using weights of one, we had put much larger weight on unused capacity and smaller weights on excess demand and unbalanced government budgets, the appropriate policy would undoubtedly call for greater government spending when the economy is in a depression. Alternatively, if most of the weight is on unbalanced budgets, the government decision-making agent would be very careful to estimate revenues and set spending as close as possible to estimated revenue in each period. The secondary goals would then influence the eventual level of government activity but they would not be of overriding importance if they called for unbalanced budgets. Clearly, the value judgments of the policy makers as to what is important have a strong bearing on their evaluations of their own best course of action.

How does one solve the policy problem as posed? What sort of rules should guide the government policy maker in his choice of r and G? To facilitate discussion of possible answers, we shall suggest a number of rules that might be followed.

1. Arbitrarily pick initial values of r and G. Whenever total potential sales exceed the firm's capacity, decrease G. If production is below full capacity, increase G when NNP is not rising. Otherwise leave G unchanged. Raise r whenever G exceeds tax revenues T, and lower r when G is less than T.

2. Let G_{t+1} differ from G_t by one-half of the difference between full capacity output and potential sales in period $t - 1$. Set r so that, given spendable income in period $t - 1$, taxes would have equaled planned government expenditures for period $t + 1$.

3. Using equation (8.5) and estimates of A and c from the consumption function, find the levels of r and G that will make equilibrium NNP

equal full capacity production and also result in a balanced budget. Denote these values of r and G by the symbols $\bar{r}$ and $\bar{G}$, respectively. (This is an interesting algebraic exercise whatever the policy eventually advocated.) Set the tax rate equal to $\bar{r}$ and government expenditures equal to $\bar{G}$, and never change them.

4. Set the tax rate as in 3, but let G_{t+1} exceed $\bar{G}$ by some fraction of the difference between full capacity NNP and actual NNP in period $t - 1$ whenever production in period $t - 1$ is below full capacity output.

These rules were not derived from a formal specification of the institutional setting, the objective, and the instruments. It is not expected that the student should do that either.

It would be interesting, however, to consider the circumstances under which each of these suggested rules would do worse than some alternative policy and to think of criticisms of these rules. Other ideas may then suggest themselves to the imaginative student. He may be able to argue why, in terms of plausible hypotheses about behavior of managers of firms, that his policy will result in a lower total penalty cost than another policy. It should become apparent in the course of the discussion that there are many facets to this problem, even in its simple setting. Each member of the class should try to imagine what he would do, beginning in month 3 in his own classroom economy, if he were given the sole responsibility of manipulating the tax rate and government expenditures under the conditions described above. Such preliminary thought should enliven the discussion about the "best" policy.

How could we resolve the question of which of two policy recommendations is really better? Each may rest on different hypotheses about behavior. Often the choice must be made on unverified beliefs or, in a real-life situation, on political realities. Over the question of how a policy would work in the setting of a classroom economy, there is a way to examine the relative merits of two different policy proposals if a controlled experiment can be set up. We are not advocating that this be done, but it is a possibility. In a real economy there is little chance for such controlled experimentation for the purpose of testing the efficacy of alternative theories.

APPENDIX TO CHAPTER 8:
DERIVATION OF SELECTED MULTIPLIERS

A number of the multiplier relationships presented in Chapter 8 require moderately extensive algebraic manipulation. This is particularly true of relationships that involve changes in the tax rates. While most of the derivations are straightforward, they do contain a number of steps. Consequently, they have been relegated to this appendix to avoid cluttering the material in Chapter 8. The notation will be the same as that employed in Section 3 of Chapter 8:

$$r = \text{original tax rate}$$
$$r' = \text{new tax rate}$$
$$Y = \text{original equilibrium net national product}$$
$$Y' = \text{new equilibrium net national product}$$

The initial equilibrium value of net national product is the following function of A, I, G, c, and r:

$$Y = \frac{A + I + G}{1 - c + cr}$$

The term $1 - c + cr = 1 - c(1 - r)$ must be positive when both c and r are between zero and one. This is assumed. Therefore, in order to have a positive equilibrium value of Y, the term $(A + I + G)$ must also be positive. These assumptions are utilized in Section 8.

If the rate is changed to r' then the new equilibrium is:

$$Y' = \frac{A + I + G}{1 - c + cr'}$$

When the economy moves from the original equilibrium to the new one, the change will be denoted by ΔY. Specifically:

$$\Delta Y = Y' - Y$$

The change in net taxes ΔT will have the following value:

$$\Delta T = r'Y' - rY$$

With these preliminaries, we can now derive the effect of a change in taxes on net national product, show that net taxes must change in the same direction as the change in tax rates, and obtain the balanced budget multiplier.

7   THE TAX-DEFICIT MULTIPLIER

If there is no change in government expenditures then the deficit increases by the amount of the decrease in net taxes:

$$\Delta D_T = -\Delta T.$$

By substitution:

$$\frac{\Delta Y}{\Delta D_T} = \frac{Y' - Y}{rY - r'Y'}$$

$$= \frac{\dfrac{A + I + G}{1 - c + cr'} - \dfrac{A + I + G}{1 - c + cr}}{\dfrac{r(A + I + G)}{1 - c + cr} - \dfrac{r'(A + I + G)}{1 - c + cr'}}$$

Multiply both numerator and denominator by $(1 - c + cr)(1 - c + cr')/$ $(A + I + G)$ to obtain:

$$\frac{\Delta Y}{\Delta D_T} = \frac{(1 - c + cr) - (1 - c + cr')}{r(1 - c + cr') - r'(1 - c + cr)}$$

$$= \frac{(r - r')c}{(r - r')(1 - c)} = \frac{c}{1 - c}$$

which is the expression shown as equation (8.9) in the text.

8   TAX-RATE CHANGES AND NET TAXES

If there is no change in A, I, G, or c, then the change in net taxes when r changes to r' is:

$$\Delta T = \frac{r'(A + I + G)}{1 - c + cr'} - \frac{r(A + I + G)}{1 - c + cr}$$

$$= \frac{(A + I + G)[r'(1 - c + cr) - r(1 - c + cr')]}{(1 - c + cr')(1 - c + cr)}$$

$$= \frac{(A + I + G)(1 - c)(r' - r)}{(1 - c + cr')(1 + c + cr)}$$

In this last expression every term in parentheses except $(r' - r)$ is positive by assumption. If tax rates have dropped so that r' is less than r, then $r' - r$ is negative and ΔT must be negative. If r' is greater than r, then ΔT must be positive. This proves the assertion that net taxes and tax rates move in the same direction barring a change in some other parameters.

9   THE BALANCED-BUDGET MULTIPLIER

Suppose government expenditures change by ΔG and tax rates are adjusted so that net taxes change by the same amount, that is, so that

$$\Delta T = \Delta G$$

By how much will equilibrium net national product change?

As a first step, add and subtract $r'Y$ to the expression for ΔT and group terms as follows:

$$\Delta T = (r' - r) Y + r' (Y' - Y)$$

This can be rewritten:

$$(r - r')Y = r'\Delta Y - \Delta T$$

and since $\Delta T = \Delta G$:

$$(r - r') Y = r'\Delta Y - \Delta G$$

Next consider the change in Y as the result of a change in *both* r and G:

$$\Delta Y = \frac{A + I + G + \Delta G}{1 - c + cr'} - Y$$

Multiply both sides by $(1 - c + cr')$

$$(1 - c + cr') \Delta Y = (A + I + G) + \Delta G - (1 - c + cr') Y$$
$$= \Delta G + (1 - c + cr) Y - (1 - c + cr') Y$$
$$= \Delta G + c(r - r') Y$$

Substitute for $(r - r') Y$ from above:

$$(1 - c + cr') \Delta Y = \Delta G + cr'\Delta Y - c\Delta G$$

and subtract $cr'\Delta Y$ from both sides:

$$(1 - c) \Delta Y = (1 - c) \Delta G.$$

Hence:

$$\Delta Y = \Delta G$$

This is the relationship mentioned in the text. The same result can be shown if the rate r is unchanged but the whole tax schedule shifts up by an amount T_o to

$$T = T_o + rY$$

If T_o is just enough to make $\Delta T = \Delta G$, then ΔY will again equal ΔG. This is left as an exercise for the interested student.

9

ADDITIONAL CONSIDERATIONS

The preceding chapters have developed a frame of reference for answering the question: What determines the level of net national product at any given time? The key concepts have been aggregate demand and the equilibrium level of net national product. Experience with a classroom economy hopefully has also helped the students appreciate why the business sector is likely to adjust production toward equilibrium and how the adjustments, through revisions of investment plans, can in turn change the temporary equilibrium. The student who has mastered these "principles of economics" is in a position to say something (however imprecise) about the likely effects on output and employment of events that alter people's spending decisions. In particular, he can understand some of the rationale for fiscal policy proposals to stimulate the economy in times of substantial unused capacity and unemployment or to depress demand that is too high relative to the economy's ability to produce goods and services.

Without going into great detail, this chapter places the elementary theory into a somewhat broader perspective. More advanced macroeconomics courses and the studies of economists are concocted from the complications that have been put aside here. Recall the simplifying assumptions that have been used to establish the classroom economy and the elementary theory of income determination: constant prices (unless in a real economy aggregate demand exceeds full capacity aggregate supply), unlimited amounts of labor available at a constant wage rate, an unchanging interest rate, and a rigid state of technology.

What would happen if these things were more flexible? This "what would happen if" question is the starting point for the curious theorist. He observes things that are not as assumed in the generally accepted theory and he wonders how the implications of the theory would be changed if some of the basic assumptions were changed.

1   MONEY, THE INTEREST RATE, AND INVESTMENT

It is commonly assumed that planned investment is influenced by the rate of interest and the general ease or difficulty of borrowing funds. If a student were to gather data on the rate of interest on various kinds of bonds, he would find that the interest rate does not stay constant. It has its ups and downs. This immediately raises the question: what causes changes in a market rate of interest? To find an answer one should look to changes in supply and demand conditions in the financial markets.

The money supply in the United States is ostensibly controlled by policies of the Federal Reserve System (often called the Fed). The Fed operates as a central bank which influences and limits the amount of money that the commercial banks, the banks that hold checking accounts, can create. Details can be found in any book on money and banking. In simpler theories, it is usually supposed that the Federal Reserve can determine precisely the amount of money. In more sophisticated versions, there are hypotheses about how the money supply depends on more specific actions of the Federal Reserve. Some theoretical formulations go so far as to hypothesize about what determines the actions of the Federal Reserve. Whatever the level of complexity, there is usually some statement about the supply of money at any given time.

Hypotheses can also be developed about the demand for money by considering why households, businesses and governments would want to hold money and asking what might influence the amount they are willing to hold. Just as he formulated a consumption function, Keynes in the *General Theory* also postulated that the demand for money is a function of the interest rate and income. We shall indicate briefly the rationale for such hypotheses.

In the discussion of the initial conditions of firms in the classroom economy, it was pointed out that a firm holds cash at the beginning of the month in order to be able to make payments to labor before the firm gets paid for the consumer goods it sells. The bigger the firm's payroll or the more such firms there are, the greater the amount of money that these businesses will hold. In general, money is needed to bridge the time gap between receipts and payments of income. This suggests (given the institutional arrangements such as paying workers every two weeks, making interest and tax payments periodically, and billing customers on a monthly basis) that the greater the total amount of production, expenditures, and income, the greater will be the amount of money that will be needed by households, businesses, and governments. For this reason, it is often hypothesized that the level of NNP influences the demand for money.

Now consider for a moment the market for bonds. When governments run deficits they issue bonds to finance the excess of expenditures over receipts. When businesses expand operations, they frequently issue bonds. Many of these bonds are negotiable; they can be sold to anyone who is willing to pay the market price. Recall that a bond is a promise to repay the amount borrowed on a specified date and to make regular interest payments in the intervening period. Suppose a bond promises to pay $50 a year for 20 years plus a principal of $1000 at the end of 20 years. If the bond sells for $1000, the buyer receives 5 percent interest. If there is a strong demand for this kind of bond, the price may rise above $1000 and any new buyer will be getting less than 5 percent interest. Conversely, if the price of the bond falls, the effective rate of interest goes up. Not only does the market price of a bond move in the opposite direction from the market rate of interest, but also if the holder of the bond sells it he may realize a gain or take a loss compared with his original purchase price.

When people accumulate savings they must also make a decision about their *portfolio*. They decide, for example, how much of their wealth to hold in the form of money, how much in the form of bonds, and how much in the form of direct ownership of a business. Suppose we concentrate on the relationship between money and bonds. Money, as defined in Chapter 2, does not earn anything for the holder, but it is safer than bonds in that bonds may fluctuate in value and there is a risk that the issuer of the bond may not be able to make the payments as promised. Intuitively, therefore, one expects that the higher the interest rate that can be earned by holding bonds, the more bonds and the less money that people will choose to hold in their portfolio. The lower the rate of interest, then, the greater the amount of money people are likely to hold; at least this is the relationship hypothesized.

At any time there is thus a supply of money and bonds and a demand for money and bonds. If, given a level of NNP, there is an interest rate that will bring the supply and demand for money and for bonds into equality, we have another example of an equilibrium condition. There are reasons to believe that it is a stable equilibrium and one that adjusts very rapidly. Suppose there is an excess supply of money at the going interest rate (supply exceeds demand). People try to use this excess money in their portfolio to buy bonds. This drives up the price of bonds and the interest rate falls. A lower interest rate will, by hypothesis, increase the quantity of money that people are willing to hold and hence the excess supply of money falls. The interest rate is thus under pressure to continue falling until the excess supply becomes zero. Conversely, when there is an excess demand for money, the interest rate can be expected to rise.

If these hypotheses hold, then any monetary policy that is directed toward a change in the money supply can also change the interest rate. For example, an increase in the supply of money may be able to drive down the rate of interest.

The decisions by businesses to invest, that is, whether or not to purchase new capital goods, must be prospective, that is, they must look to the future; and an important consideration is the expected profitability of the ventures over the useful life of the productive assets. This requires anticipations of future demand, prices, and the costs of associated inputs. If there is a strong likelihood that all costs can easily be covered including the cost of borrowing the funds to finance the project, then the investment is very likely to be made. If there appears to be a fairly narrow profit margin, the cost of borrowing may become crucial. When the interest rate is low an investment project may be undertaken that might not be deemed worthwhile if the interest costs were higher. These very brief considerations suggest the hypothesis that the level of planned investment may be higher the lower the interest rate. If so, then monetary policy may be able to influence aggregate demand through its effect on investment.

By forcing the market rate of interest alternately to rise and fall, monetary policy undoubtedly influences the timing of investment. If interest rates are high and money is "tight" many projects may be postponed until interest rates are lower and money becomes "easier." Thus, in periods of apparent excess aggregate demand, monetary policy may be able to cut down on the demand by making it more costly for businesses, and for that matter, governments and households, to borrow the funds necessary to make major purchases. As indicated in the discussion of fiscal policy, there may be some difficulties in timing here. High interest rates and tight money may have their full impact on demand possibly six months to a year later.

2　OTHER COMPLICATIONS

So far labor markets have been largely disregarded. It has been assumed that there is an adequate supply of labor, that is, that there are more people willing and able to work than businesses are willing to employ, at the going wages. Any such excess supply of labor is called *unemployment*. Full employment of labor in the United States is believed to occur when only 3 or 4 percent of the people in the labor force do not have jobs. If the unemployment rate gets up to 6 or 7 percent, the labor market is clearly in disequilibrium. If it were observed that wages tended readily to fall in such circumstances, macroeconomic theory would need to take this into account. Since wages do not go down when there is less than full employment, the assumption of rigid wages in the short run appears to be a plausible characterization of the present U.S. economy.[1]

Conceivably institutions could be devised to promote greater wage flexibility if this could be demonstrated as an effective way to eliminate unemployment quickly. Suppose there is unemployment; and suppose there is a lower wage rate at which businesses, in the expectation of selling everything produced at the present prices, would hire everyone who is willing and able to work. What would happen if wages were cut to this level? Suppose as a result that businesses temporarily increased employment and production. Real net national product would go up; but if demand rose by less than the increase in NNP, as it will with an MPC less than one, then businesses would accumulate unwanted inventories. In that case, they would either cut back employment and production or cut prices or both. If the lower prices discourage maintaining the extra employment, then the excess supply of labor will reappear except at lower wages and prices.

Unless the lower wages and prices somehow stimulate sufficient aggregate demand, businesses are not going to maintain a higher level of production just because wages are lower. There are situations, that we shall not develop here, in which lower prices and wages could result in sufficient increases in aggregate demand; but since the same objective, eliminating unemployment, can be accomplished more easily by appropriate monetary and fiscal policies, most economists do not advocate wage cuts as a policy for achieving full employment.

Employment generally refers to the utilization of the available labor supply. Section 5 in Chapter 7 considered the inflationary potential created by situations when aggregate demand exceeds full capacity supply, that is, the supply when the stock of investment goods is fully utilized. Can an economy be at full capacity and not at full employment, or vice versa? Theoretically either is possible, but nearly full employment and nearly full capacity usually occur simultaneously, and capacity utilization generally slips when unemployment grows. This phenomenon can be explained by a fairly rigid link between employment of labor and utilization of plant and equipment in the short run and a greater flexibility in the long run when managers plan the type of productive process they wish to install. Thus, adjustments in the labor market may influence both aggregate demand and aggregate supply.

The foregoing considerations indicate how a simple theory can be expanded to take account of complexities that are observed to exist in

---

[1]Wages did fall in the United States in the early 1930s, but we do not envision a return to the massive unemployment that characterized the Great Depression.

a real economy. But the general frame of reference is not necessarily changed. Output and employment are still largely determined by aggregate demand and aggregate supply. The monetary policies of the Federal Reserve, for example, are believed to work through their influence on aggregate demand.

There are, of course, many other complications. Aggregate adjustments are the result of many individual decisions, and in a complex economy different industries and different people are not affected in the same way at the same time. It is therefore a legitimate exercise for an economist to wonder what difference it would make in his theory if he assumed a multiplicity of products, different kinds of labor skills, or many types of financial securities. Can understanding be enhanced by such a disaggregated approach and will the aggregate theory still hold? Do changes in total government expenditures, for example, change total employment in a predictable way? Unless it can be demonstrated that many parts of the economy operate in extreme isolation from other parts, the aggregative theory makes sense, but this assertion remains undocumented here.

3 SPEED OF ADJUSTMENT AND FISCAL POLICY

In addition to complications arising out of a great variety of products, there are complexities connected with the time dimension. How rapidly does an economy adjust toward a temporary equilibrium, and how quickly does the equilibrium change? In an introductory text this sort of question cannot be pursued at length. There are, however, a few observations that can be made on the basis of the analysis so far.

In the classroom economy producers can make substantial changes from one month to the next, so that large changes in NNP are possible within a few months. Imagine how much slower the changes would be if the limit to the change in materials ordered were a change of 2 units from one month to the next instead of 20 units. In that case, it would take at least 10 months for a firm to change its level of monthly materials ordered by 20 units. The adjustment would be even slower if the limit were a change of one unit per month. Only moderate changes would then be observed in production, income, and sales. While equilibrium might not bounce around so much, it might also be a matter of two or three years before the economy caught an equilibrium originally shifted up by a major increase in the aggregate demand schedule.

In the U.S. economy, decisions are not all made in synchronized jumps and many decisions are routine and repetitive. A company which schedules its production a month in advance may also try to keep its level of production reasonably constant from one month to the next. In that case its orders from suppliers will not go through violent changes (unless a major strike takes place or is imminent). This enables the suppliers to maintain reasonably constant levels of production. If final demand picks up, it may be met out of inventories, and production only gradually stepped up. Furthermore, different companies plan production schedules at different intervals. Thus, any one firm making a large change by itself has a minor impact. When producers neither desire nor anticipate rapid adjustments in production, only moderate changes in production will occur from one month to the next.

What is the extent of changes of aggregate production in the U.S. economy? Referring to Figure 7.3, one can see that the greatest percentage decreases in (constant dollar) GNP occurred during the Great Depression and right after World War II. The biggest percentage increases occurred during World War II. There was also a rapid increase in the early to middle 1960s. Even in these periods of most rapid change, the monthly changes were not great on the average. From 1929 to 1932 the average monthly decline in GNP was less than one percent. During the postwar reconversion from 1945 to 1946 the average monthly decline was approximately 1.1 percent. During World War II the average monthly increase in GNP was about one percent per month. In the expansion from 1964 to 1966 GNP increased on the average about 0.7 percent per month. Thus, the greatest aggregate changes in the U.S. economy have been less than at a rate that would occur in the classroom economy if orders and production were changed by no more than one unit per firm per month.

Changes in the classroom economy are allowed to occur with much greater rapidity than any observed aggregate changes in the U.S. economy. Greater potential volatility in the classroom economy avoids highly repetitive decisions period after period. While the process of adjustment has some similarities to adjustments in the U.S. economy, the speed with which they occur is very much different.

These relatively slow adjustments in the U.S. economy may be either a hindrance or a help to effective policy manipulation. They are a hindrance if economists are seldom sure where the economy is, relative to equilibrium. As an example, there may be substantial unemployment and excess capacity while the temporary equilibrium is already above the full capacity level of aggregate supply. A fiscal policy stimulus to aggregate demand may have the effect of eliminating unemployment more quickly than without the stimulus. At the same time such a policy can aggravate subsequent inflationary pressures if the government is unwilling or unable to undertake rapid changes in its fiscal policy measures.

If the political climate is such that rapid changes in policy measures are feasible, the relatively slow adjustment by the rest of the economy may be a help to policy. The government may freely adjust its policies. If there is an excess supply of labor (unemployment), an increase in government spending or a tax cut can safely help to reduce unemployment more quickly. At early signs of inflation a policy reversal can then pull down aggregate demand and successfully remove the inflationary pressures. As soon as production begins to level off or head down, another reversal can quickly avoid a depression.

We leave it an open question whether the political climate will allow and the impact of fiscal measures is rapid enough (relative to other changes) for the U.S. government to be able to use policy measures to steer the economy along a path that keeps down both inflation and unemployment. In this regard it is an interesting exercise to examine carefully the U.S. economy during the period from 1963 to the present. How effective have government fiscal policies been? In retrospect, are there any policies that should have been different?

4   A FASCINATING PUZZLE

In connection with the classroom economy, each student has been asked to act as the manager of a firm, to figure out how to make the greatest possible profits for his firm. He has been asked to wear a more important hat as well — that of a student of economics. His main problem has been to explain the level of economic activity at any given time.

For the fun of it, consider an analogy to this problem. Imagine being confronted with the task of putting together an extraordinary jigsaw puzzle. There are thousands of pieces on a huge table. Can enough of the pieces be assembled for an observer to perceive the panorama depicted by the completed puzzle? There are a number of difficulties. The puzzle keeps growing at one end as new pieces are fashioned and scattered on the table. A large number of useless pieces appear to be mixed in with the ones needed, but it is hard to tell whether or not a piece is useless. Furthermore, there may be a number of important pieces missing.

To add to the difficulties, there are numerous kibitzers, and their advice often conflicts. Some of them pick up a few pieces and describe in elaborate detail the colors, textures, and patterns to be found on each selected piece. They claim that doing the same with enough pieces will eventually enable one to say something about the bigger picture even if no one ever figures out how to put the pieces together. These people are analogous to descriptive or institutional economists who have little interest in or respect for theory.

There are others who take a few pieces that attract their attention and proceed to draw a neat picture of their own around these pieces. They say that there is no need to find where the pieces fit since their picture is sufficient to understand what the completed panorama would be like if it were ever completed. This approach is analogous to that of pure theorists who have little if any concern with what goes on in a real economy, except for a few superficial observations.

The point of this analogy should be clear. Without some way of organizing pieces of evidence and developing criteria for judging whether or not evidence is relevant, economists are unlikely to make much progress. To understand what determines net national product, it is fruitless to do no more than recite the magnitude of everything. It would also be largely irrelevant to do nothing more than fabricate a hypothetical picture of the way the economy works. Both description and theory are indispensable, but they are not sufficient. The really difficult, and yet essential, step is to make sure that a theory does explain the events that occur, that is, find the pieces that fit and ascertain how the new part of the picture, the growing end of the puzzle, is being created.

An explanation that is not contradicted by actual events can be most useful for analyzing the causes and cures of depressions or inflations, for making greater profits on the basis of this knowledge, for suggesting measures that will assure continued expansion, or for evaluating the short- and long-run impact of such things as wage changes, technological changes, or interest rate changes. However, executives, members of legislative bodies, and advisers who influence and make policy decisions on economic matters must act even if the whole picture is only dimly or imperfectly seen. They use those hypotheses or theories that they believe are most in accord with the way things happen. It is the task of economists to sift the evidence objectively and convey to policy makers and the public the clearest possible view of the overall picture.

APPENDIX

A SAMPLE FORTRAN PROGRAM FOR HANDLING THE COMPUTATIONS OF A CLASSROOM ECONOMY

The following program is set to handle 10 firms and provide computations for as many as 20 periods at a time. The number of firms can be increased by changing the dimension cards. The output consists of a page for each firm showing its decisions, inventory holdings, retained earnings, and data from the classroom economy. For the instructor there is a page for each period showing what every firm has done.

The deck of input data cards are ordered as follows:
1. Header card
2. Second card
3. Carryover cards
4. Decision cards

If the computations for more than one classroom economy are run at once, repeat this sequence for each economy. A blank card at the end will terminate the computations. The card formats are as follows:

Header Card

columns
1– 3 Economy number
4– 6 Number of firms
7– 8 Type of consumption function (1 for type I, etc.)
9–12 A-term in the consumption function

columns
13–16 b-term in the consumption function
17–20 D-term in the consumption function (if type III)
21–24 Maximum allowable production
25–28 Maximum allowable change in materials ordered

Second Card

columns
1– 3 Economy number
4– 6 First period (FP) to be computed this run
7– 9 Last period (LP) to be computed this run
10–12 Random number (if any) in computing potential sales for period LP

columns
13–15 Potential sales in period FP
16–18 Potential sales in period FP $+$ 1
19–21 Potential sales in period FP $+$ 2
. . . and so on for as many as 20 periods if desired

Carryover cards
(one for each firm)

columns
1– 3 Economy number
4– 6 Period number (FP)
7– 9 Firm number

columns
10–12 Inventories of materials
13–15 Inventories of finished goods

152

16–18   Materials ordered in previous period (FP − 1)

19–25   Cumulative retained earnings
26–31   Spendable income in previous period

Decision cards

columns
1– 3   Economy number
4– 6   Period number
7– 9   N1, number of first firm with decisions on this card
10–12   N2, number of last firm with decisions on this card
13–16   Units produced by firm N1

columns
17–19   Materials ordered by firm N1
20–22   Units produced by firm N1 + 1
23–25   Materials ordered by firm N1 + 1
  . . .   and so on for as many as ten firms on a card

The header card provides information about the number of firms, the consumption function, and limits on production and change in orders.

The second card allows the records for several periods to be processed at once. If potential sales have already been announced for a period, this figure can be punched into the second card, and will be used for preparing the accounts. If it is not punched the computer will figure potential sales for that period. The second card also allows for a random number to be inserted into the final figure for potential sales. If only one period is being processed it is still necessary to have a second card. The same period number should be punched for both FP and LP.

The program calls for the carryover cards to be punched out by the computer for use in a continuing run. For the first period that the classroom economy is in operation, only one carryover card is needed. This should contain the period number 1, the firm number 1, and the beginning inventories of materials and finished goods assigned to each and every firm.

A decision card has been set up so that one period's decisions by 10 firms can be punched on one card. If it is found that errors arise with this format, it is easy to change the program to accept one decision card per firm per period.

```
C     PROGRAM TO PERFORM CALCULATIONS FOR THE CLASSROOM ECONOMY
C
      PROGRAM MAIN(INPUT,OUTPUT,PUNCH,TAPE5=INPUT,
     *            TAPE6=OUTPUT,TAPE7=PUNCH)
      DIMENSION FG(20,10),HM(20,10),Q(20,10),R(20,10),S(20,10),
     *PROF(20,10),CUM(20,10),PS(20),CT(20),YT(20),HT(20),
     *WT(20),Z(20),RT(20),TQ(20),TR(20),TM(20),TFG(20),RX(20)
C
C     READ HEADER CARD
C
    3 READ(5,501) IE,NF,JTYPE,AA,BB,DD,QMAX,RMAX
  501 FORMAT(2I3,I2,5F4.0)
      IF(IE.EQ.0) STOP
      XNF=NF
C
C     READ SECOND CARD
C
      READ(5,503) JE,JP,LP,RAND,(PS(M),M=1,20)
  503 FORMAT (3I3,23F3.0)
      IF(JE.NE.IE) GO TO 299
      MM=LP-JP+1
C
C     READ CARRYOVER CARDS
C
      DO 18 K=1,NF
      READ(5,505) JE,JP,NJ,HM(1,NJ),FG(1,NJ),RX(NJ),CUM(1,NJ),ZLAST
  505 FORMAT(3I3,3F3.0,2F6.0)
      IF(JE.NE.IE) GO TO 299
      IF(JP.GT.1) GO TO 18
      DO 15 J=2,NF
      FG(1,J)=FG(1,1)
      HM(1,J)=HM(1,1)
      RX(J)=HM(1,J)
   15 CUM(1,J)=0
      RX(1)=HM(1,1)
      GO TO 23
   18 CONTINUE
C
C     READ DECISION CARDS
C
   23 M=0
      NCC=(NF+9)/10
   26 KOUNT=0
      M=M+1
      TFG(M)=0
      TM(M)=0
      TQ(M)=0
      TR(M)=0
      DO 28 K=1,NCC
      READ (5,507) JE,NP,N1,N2,(Q(M,J),R(M,J),J=N1,N2)
  507 FORMAT (4I3,20F3.0)
      NN=NP-M+1
      IF(JP.NE.NN) GO TO 298
      IF(JE.NE.IE) GO TO 298
   28 KOUNT=KOUNT+N2-N1 + 1
      IF(KOUNT.NE.NF) GO TO 298
```

```
      DO 31 J=1,NF
      IF(Q(M,J).GT.HM(M,J)) Q(M,J)=HM(M,J)
      IF(Q(M,J).GT.QMAX) Q(M,J)=QMAX
      IF(R(M,J).GT.(RX(J)+RMAX)) R(M,J)=RX(J)+RMAX
      IF(R(M,J).LT.(RX(J)-RMAX)) R(M,J)=RX(J)-RMAX
      RX(J)=R(M,J)
      TM(M)=TM(M)+HM(M,J)
      TFG(M)=TFG(M)+FG(M,J)
      TQ(M)=TQ(M)+Q(M,J)
   31 TR(M)=TR(M)+R(M,J)
C
C     COMPUTE POTENTIAL SALES,CONSUMPTION AND PROFITS
C
      PN=NP
      Z(M)= .5*(TQ(M)+TR(M))
      IF(PS(M).GT.0.) GO TO 38
   34 ZZ=Z(M)
      IF(JTYPE.EQ.2) ZZ=ZLAST
      ZLAST=Z(M)
      KD = (AA+ BB*ZZ + DD*PN)/XNF + RAND + .5
      PS(M)=KD
   38 CT(M)=0
      DO 41 J=1,NF
      S(M,J)= PS(M)
      AVAIL = FG(M,J)+Q(M,J)
      IF(PS(M).GT.AVAIL) S(M,J)=AVAIL
      CT(M)=CT(M)+S(M,J)
      FG(M+1,J)= AVAIL-S(M,J)
      HM(M+1,J)= HM(M,J)+R(M,J)-Q(M,J)
      DIVD=10.*PS(M)
      PROF(M,J)=50.*S(M,J) -HM(M,J) -2.*FG(M,J)-2700.-DIVD
      CUM(M+1,J)=CUM(M,J)+PROF(M,J)
   41 CONTINUE
C
C     COMPUTE CLASSROOM INCOME DATA
C
      YT(M)=.4*(TQ(M)+TR(M))+ .2*CT(M)
      HT(M)=YT(M)-CT(M)
      WT(M)= 8.*XNF +.2*TR(M)+ .4*TQ(M)
      RT(M)=YT(M)-WT(M)
      IF(M.LT.MM) GO TO 26
C
C     WRITE OUT RECORDS FOR INDIVIDUAL FIRMS
C
      DO 65 J=1,NF
      WRITE(6,601) IE,J
  601 FORMAT(1H1,30X,7HECONOMY,I4,30X,4HFIRM,I4///
     1      50X,26RECORD OF FIRM DECISIONS    //
     2      10X,50H    MONTH    MATERIALS    ORDER    FIN GDS    PROD ,
     3      40H  P SALES  UNITS SOLD  RET EARN    CUM )
      DO 55 M=1,MM
      KM=JP+M-1
      WRITE(6,603)KM,HM(M,J),R(M,J),FG(M,J),Q(M,J),PS(M),S(M,J),
     1      PROF(M,J),CUM(M+1,J)
  603 FORMAT(1H0,14X,I4,8F10.0)
   55 CONTINUE
```

```
      WRITE(6,605) CUM(MM+1,J),HM(MM+1,J),FG(MM+1,J)
  605 FORMAT(1H0,9X,18HCUMULATIVE PROFIT= ,F8.0//
     1        10X,25HMATERIALS FOR NEXT MONTH= ,F5.0//
     2        10X,26HFINISHED GOODS NEXT MONTH= , F5.0////)
      WRITE(6,607)
  607 FORMAT(1H0,49X,25HCLASSROOM INCOME ACCOUNTS// 10X,
     1 60H      MONTH    WAGES   PROFITS      CONS    INVEST        NNP
     2    11H  SPEND INC )
      DO 65 M=1,MM
      KM=JP+M-1
      WRITE(6,609) KM,WT(M),RT(M),CT(M),HT(M),YT(M),Z(M)
  609 FORMAT(1H0,15X,I4,6F10.1)
   65 CONTINUE
C
C     WRITE OUT INSTRUCTORS RECORD
C
      DO 77 M=1,MM
      KM=JP+M-1
      WRITE(6,611) IE,KM
  611 FORMAT(1H1,30X,7HECONOMY,I4,30X,5HMONTH,I4///
     1        30X,26HRECORD OF FIRM DECISIONS   //
     2      10X,50H      FIRM  MATERIALS      ORDER      FIN GDS      PROD
     3      40H  P SALES  UNITS SOLD   RET EARN      CUM )
      WRITE(6,612) (J,HM(M,J),R(M,J),FG(M,J),Q(M,J),PS(M),
     1              S(M,J), PROF(M,J),CUM(M+1,J),J=1,NF)
  612 FORMAT(16X,I4,8F10.0)
      WRITE(6,614) TM(M),TR(M),TFG(M),TQ(M),CT(M)
  614 FORMAT(1H0,13X,6HTOTALS,4F10.0,10X,F10.0//)
      WRITE(6,607)
      WRITE(6,609) KM,WT(M),RT(M),CT(M),HT(M),YT(M),Z(M)
   77 CONTINUE
C
C     PUNCH CARRYOVER CARDS FOR NEXT RUN
C
      JP=JP+MM
      LAST=ZLAST
      DO 66 J=1,NF
      LLA =HM(MM+1,J)
      LLB =FG(MM+1,J)
      LLC =RX(J)
      LLD =CUM(MM+1,J)
      WRITE(7,705) JE,JP,J,LLA ,LLB ,LLC ,LLD LAST
  705 FORMAT(6I3,2I6,49X,1H3)
   66 CONTINUE
      GO TO 3
C
C     STOP IF CARDS IMPROPERLY ORDERED OR NUMBERED
C
  298 WRITE(6,801)
  801 FORMAT(35HIDECISION CARDS IMPROPERLY ORDERED )
      STOP
  299 WRITE(6,803)
  803 FORMAT(46H1HEADER OR CARRYOVER CARDS IMPROPERLY ORDERED )
      STOP
      END
```

SUGGESTED REFERENCES

National Income Accounting
*Ackley, Gardner, *Macroeconomic Theory*. New York: Macmillan, 1961, pp. 25-101.
National Bureau of Economic Research, *A Critique of the U.S. Income and Product Accounts*, Studies in Income and Wealth, vol. 22. Princeton, N.J.: Princeton University Press, 1958.
*Shapiro, Edward, *Macroeconomic Analysis*. New York: Harcourt, Brace, 1966, pp. 13-134.
Studenski, Paul, *The Income of Nations*. New York: New York University Press, 1958.
U.S. Office of Business Economics, *National Income, 1954 Edition*, A Supplement to the Survey of Current Business. Washington, D.C.: U.S. Government Printing Office, 1954.
U.S. Office of Business Economics, *U.S. Income and Output*, A Supplement to the Survey of Current Business. Washington, D.C.: U.S. Government Printing Office, 1958.

Economic Analysis and Policy
*Bailey, Martin J., *National Income and the Price Level*. New York: McGraw-Hill, 1962.
Committee for Economic Development, *Fiscal and Monetary Policy for High Employment*. New York, 1962.
Denison, E. F., *The Sources of Economic Growth in the United States and the Alternatives Before Us*. New York: Committee for Economic Development, 1962.
*Dernburg, T. F. and D. M. McDougall, *Macroeconomics*, 3rd ed. New York: McGraw-Hill, 1968.
Friedman, M. and W. W. Heller, *Monetary vs. Fiscal Policy*. New York: Norton, 1969.
Hansen, A., *A Guide to Keynes*. New York: McGraw-Hill, 1953.
*Keiser, N., *Macroeconomics, Fiscal Policy, and Economic Growth*. New York: John Wiley, 1964.
Keynes, J. M., *The General Theory of Employment, Interest and Money*. New York: Harcourt, Brace, 1936.
Leijonhufvud, Axel, *Of Keynesian Economics and the Economics of Keynes*. New York: Oxford University Press, 1968.
Lindauer, John, ed., *Macroeconomic Readings*. New York: Free Press, 1968.
*Lindauer, John, *Macroeconomics*. New York: John Wiley, 1968.
Mathews, R. C. O., *The Business Cycle*. Chicago: University of Chicago Press, 1959.
*McKenna, Joseph P., *Aggregate Economic Analysis*, 3rd ed. New York: Holt, Rinehart and Winston, Inc., 1969.
Mueller, M. G., ed., *Readings in Macroeconomics*. New York: Holt, Rinehart and Winston, Inc., 1966.
Tobin, James, *National Economic Policy*. New Haven, Conn.: Yale University Press, 1966.
U.S. Council of Economic Advisers, *Annual Report of the Council of Economic Advisers*. Washington, D.C.: U.S. Government Printing Office.

Experimental Economics
Carlson, J. A., "The Stability of an Experimental Market with a Supply-Response Lag," *Southern Economic Journal*, Vol. 33, January 1967, pp. 305-321.

*Textbooks are marked with an asterisk

158 *Suggested References*

Fouraker, L. M. and S. Siegel, *Bargaining Behavior.* New York: McGraw-Hill, 1963.

Haldi, J. and H. M. Wagner, *Simulated Economic Models: A Laboratory Guide to Economic Principles of Market Behavior.* Homewood, Ill.: Irwin, 1963.

Luce, R. D. and H. Raiffa, *Games and Decisions.* New York: John Wiley, 1957.

Siegel, S. and L. M. Fouraker, *Bargaining and Group Decision Making: Experiments in Bilateral Monopoly.* New York: McGraw-Hill, 1960.

Smith, V. L., "An Experimental Study of Competitive Market Behavior," *Journal of Political Economy,* Vol. 70, April 1962, pp. 111-137.

Smith, V. L., "Experimental Auction Markets and the Walrasian Hypothesis," *Journal of Political Economy,* Vol. 73, August 1965, pp. 387-393.

Symposium on Experimental Economics, *Review of Economic Studies,* To be published.

INDEX

spendable, 65, 72
  data on, 86
Income accounting, *see* National income
  accounting
Income accounts, *see* Classroom income
  accounts
Income determination, theory of, 6–7,
  50–60, 92, 93, 119, 130, 143
Income statement, 13–14, 21–22, 28
Indirect business taxes, 40–41
Individual behavior, economic theory and,
  4–5
Inferences, graphical, consumer behavior,
  86–90
Inflation, 108–109, 132, 150
Inflationary pressures, 108, 150
Institutional setting, 135
Instruments, 135
Interaction, 79
Interest, 11, 23, 145
  rate of, 23, 145–146
Inventories, 25
  business, change in, 38
Inventory holding costs, 23–24, 27
Inventory investment, 27–29
  in the U.S. economy (1929–1968), 116
Investment, 8, 146
  capacity-creating effect of, 110
  demand-generating effect of, 110
  fixed, 38, 104, 116
  gross, 36
  growth and, 110–112
  inventory, 27–29, 116
  net, 36
  planned, 94–95
Investment decision, 8
Investment goods, 7–8
  consumer goods and, distinction between,
    35
  markets for, 10–11
Investment plans, dynamic adjustments and,
  98–104
Keynes, John Maynard, 50, 51, 53, 144
Labor markets, 11, 146–147
Liabilities, 26
  long-term, 26
  short-term, 26
  total, 26
Liabilities-plus-net-worth side of the balance
  sheet, 24–25
Long-term liabilities, 26
Macroeconomics, 3
  theory of, 3, 4–5, 12, 19
Managers, 8
Marginal propensity to consume (MPC),
  53, 82, 104, 123, 147
Markets, 8–12
  buyers and sellers, necessity for, 8–9

consumer goods, 10
  financial, 11–12
  investment goods, 10–11
  labor, 11, 146–147
Materials, 19
  inventories of, 25
Microeconomics, 3
Money, 10, 144–145
Month, period length in classroom
  economy, 19–20
Multipliers, 55–60, 96–97
  balanced-budget, 128–129, 141–142
  derivation of, 139–142
  government, 124–129
  government expenditures, 125–128
  tax-deficit, 140–141
Musgrave, Richard, 131
National income, 40, 41
  product accounts and, 38–41
National income accounting, 32–49
  classroom income accounts, 43, 46–49
  disposable income, real NNP and, 41–43
  financial data for the classroom economy,
    additional, 45–46
  gross national product (GNP), 37–38,
    41
  national income, product accounts and,
    38–41
  net national product (NNP), 33–37, 38,
    40, 41
  real NNP, disposable income and, 41–43,
    48
  value added, 43–45, 46
Net earnings, 22, 29
Net exports, 38
Net investment, 36
Net national product (NNP), 33–37, 38, 40,
  41, 50, 55, 94, 102, 107, 109, 110, 114,
  121, 124, 130, 131, 145, 147, 148
  equilibrium, 57, 58, 122, 143
  real, 42–43, 48, 138, 147
    disposable income and, 41–43
Net taxes, 121
Net value added, 44
Net worth, 26
Opportunity cost, 23 n.
Period, the, in classroom economy, 19
Period analysis, 14–16, 19–20
Planned investment, 94–95
Potential sales, 61, 71, 79
  computing, record keeping and, 71–76
Portfolio, 145
Prices, 9, 20
  constant, 143
  in the U.S. economy (1929–1968), indexes
    of, 117
Product accounts, national income and,
  38–41